SHUT UP,
STOP WHINING,
AND GET A LIFE

SHUT UP,
STOP WHINING,
AND GET A LIFE

A KICK-BUTT APPROACH
TO A BETTER LIFE

SECOND EDITION, REVISED & UPDATED

LARRY WINGET

WILEY

John Wiley & Sons, Inc.

Published by John Wiley & Sons, Inc., Hoboken, New Jersey.
Published simultaneously in Canada.

Comic panels are printed with permission from SmarterComics, LLC and Writers of the Round Table Press Inc.; illustrations by Shane Clester.

For general information on our other products and services or for technical support, please contact our Customer Care Department within the United States at (800) 762-2974, outside the United States at (317) 572-3993 or fax (317) 572-4002.

Wiley also publishes its books in a variety of electronic formats. Some content that appears in print may not be available in electronic books. For more information about Wiley products, visit our website at www.wiley.com.

Library of Congress Cataloging-in-Publication Data:

Winget, Larry.
    Shut up, stop whining, and get a life : a kick-butt approach to a better life / Larry Winget. – 2nd ed., rev. & updated.
        p. cm.
    ISBN 978-1-118-02451-5 (pbk.); ISBN 978-1-118-07813-6 (ebk);
    ISBN 978-1-118-07812-9 (ebk); ISBN 978-1-118-07811-2 (ebk)
    1. Life skills–Handbooks, manuals, etc.   2. Conduct of life.   3. Success.   I. Title.
    HQ2037.W57 2011
    646.7–dc22

                                                                                    2011001513

Printed in the United States of America.

10   9   8   7   6   5   4   3   2   1

I lovingly dedicate this book to all of the crap that ever happened to me. It has made me who I am today. It caused me to read, to search, to pay attention, to learn, to listen, to accept, to grow, to take responsibility, and to create a life I am proud to call mine.

Without all of that crap, I would be like 99.9 percent of the world: leading a life of mediocrity, full of blame, resentment, and whining.

I needed every bit of that crap to happen to me because, without it, this book wouldn't exist for you to read and there would be no reason for you to listen to me.

CONTENTS

PREFACE

"Just have a positive attitude and everything will be okay."
"As long as you feel really good about yourself, everything
　　will be terrific!"
"The key to happiness and success is to be yourself."
"You can attract all of the success and money to you that you
　　will ever need."

Heard that stuff before? Of course you have. All over the world
you find people shouting that drivel from books, stages, and the
airwaves. The Internet is full of it! All of the gurus will tell you
just be happy, be yourself, and sit back and think your way to
success and prosperity. What a happy load of crap!

My message isn't like that. I'm not into cute little sayings
or platitudes or much of the other stuff the motivational gurus/
bozos are saying. I don't care whether you have a positive attitude
or a negative attitude. In fact, I'm more in favor of the negative attitude, as you will soon discover. And I don't care if you
feel good about yourself or care much about how you feel about
anything. Feel, feel, feel—doesn't anybody *do* anything anymore?
Not really.

People buy into all of this happy crap because the people
sound good, and they make you feel good. The problem is, they
don't produce many tangible results. Then folks get frustrated
and disillusioned and end up abandoning their pursuit of being

more, doing more, and having more. They become complacent and settle for less than they have to. Some even become bitter and just quit trying. Sound familiar?

Here is my bottom line message. The message you need to understand going in.

Your life is your own damn fault!

Welcome to my world. No excuses allowed. Just go to the mirror, look yourself in the eye, and say to your own face, "This is all my own damn fault!"

No real success can be achieved until you accept the fact that your life is your own fault. You are responsible. Your thoughts, words, and actions created the life you are living. Even on the outside chance that something horrible happened to you that you had nothing to do with, how you react to that event is still your fault. What you do about it is your fault. It's always your fault. Once you understand that and take responsibility for your life at every level, you will begin to achieve success.

That stance is what makes my approach different from others in the personal development industry. (That plus the earrings and the shirts and the boots!) I don't believe in blaming or making excuses, and I won't listen to your whining, complaining, or pointing the finger of blame anywhere other than your own face. You may think that is a mean, heartless approach but I assure you it isn't. It's an approach that is rooted in caring and truth and reality. I care enough to tell you the truth so you will face reality.

That's why I wrote this book and why I am so excited that you are reading this new revised edition of my first bestselling book. This *Wall Street Journal* #1 bestseller is the book that started it all for me and set me apart from all of the warm and fuzzy pat-you-on-the-head-and-tell-you-it's-all-going-to-be-okay motivational books on the market. The success of this hardcore self-help book led me to write four other bestsellers: *It's Called Work for a Reason*; *You're Broke Because You Want to Be*; *People Are Idiots and I Can Prove It*; and *Your Kids Are Your Own Fault*.

My goal in writing this book is not to make you feel better. My goal is to remind you to go to the only place in the world where you can lay blame: the mirror. And it will give you a simple, easy-to-follow plan that can point you in the direction of success, happiness, and prosperity.

The book is divided into three parts:

Shut Up! Chances are you are talking too much and need to listen. Or as my Dad used to tell me: "You're broadcasting when you ought to be tuned in."

Stop Whining! Wallowing in your problems doesn't fix your problems so stop complaining, blaming, griping, bitching, moaning and groaning, and take responsibility for your life.

Get a Life! Create the life you want to have by living by design and not by default. Make a decision, create a plan, and then go to work to make that plan come to life.

Simple? Of course! Easy? Not always. Worth it? Absolutely. This book is tough. It's meant to be. I want to shake you up and wake you up. I want to make you mad. I want to make you sick of accepting less than the best for yourself. I want you to become disgusted with your life, and I want to create in you an intense desire to have more, do more, and most of all, become more. I want you to see that you can create the life you want. I want you to have it all. But in order to do that I may have to kick your butt and tick you off a little along the way.

For some of you my approach may seem harsh, but some of you will barely be disturbed. It just depends on where you are in your life. If someone is deeply asleep, sometimes you have to shake that person very hard to make him fully awake. If he is just dozing, a little nudge will be enough. For some of you this book will be your nudge. For others, it will be a rude awakening—a slap in the face—a kick in the butt.

My style is confrontational. You've probably figured that out already. I am caustic and abrupt and call it like I see it. I don't have time to be tactful. You don't have time for me to be tactful either. However, my confrontational style by itself would only make you mad. Now let's get clear on this: I'm not afraid of making you mad. In fact, I enjoy that a bit. Because if you get a little mad, that means you are willing to be challenged. And while you are being challenged, you can consider my suggestions for how to live a better life. While the style of writing is confrontational and in-your-face, my motive is to make you mad enough that you will do whatever it takes to accomplish whatever you want in life. Then I'll tell you what it takes.

This book isn't going to be like the other self-help books you have read, unless you have read other books by me. The personal development marketplace wouldn't tolerate this kind of abuse as a rule. I think most of the books on the market today just help people suffer in comfort. They are a pacifier for the most part. They want you to believe that regardless of how much your life sucks, that is okay; there are plenty of conditions that were beyond your control that led you to that condition. Those books sometimes do nothing but help you coat yourself in a shell that serves no purpose except to make it harder for the real truth—I mean the ugly truth—to get in. My goal isn't to help you suffer in comfort. My goal is to break through that shell to offer you some truths that will change your perspective, make you think, and alter your results. The way I do that is by getting in your face and shaking you up a bit in order to wake you up from the sleep of mediocrity.

It's pretty much like the mule and the two-by-four theory: You have to get the mule's attention first with the two-by-four in order to get him to do something. Consider this book to be the two-by-four in your life.

I don't want to mislead you by seeming to be high and mighty or by pretending to have mastered everything it takes to be successful. I haven't. I don't know it all. There was a time not so long ago when I did think that I knew it all. That was just plain stupid. Now I am fully aware that the more you really do know, the more you realize you don't know. So like you, I'm still learning too. I haven't even truly mastered all of what I talk about in these pages. Unlike others who write books and give speeches saying they have mastered all they speak of and write about, I would rather be honest and just tell you I am a mess like everyone else in this world. I am just doing the best I can with what I have learned until I can learn a little more and then do a little better. Actually, that's all I am suggesting you do as well. Learn a little from this writing and do the best you can with it until you learn a little more and can do a little better.

Therefore, I openly admit to you right now I don't know everything there is to know about being successful or getting rich or being healthy or anything else, really.

But this book isn't about what I don't know; it's about what I do know. I am absolutely sure of the things in this book. The things I talk about in this book are the result of thousands of hours spent reading thousands of books and listening to others on CD and DVD, and many years of gaining personal experience by living life the hard way—by screwing up and, every once in a while, doing things right as well. This is real world stuff. This stuff works.

This book isn't an end-all be-all book. It's just a starting place. In fact, consider this Book One in my series of books. I can't cover everything in just one book. So for those of you who read this book and want to know more about any of the topics covered, the good news is you can. But, don't be too concerned that you won't get what you need out of this one; this book has plenty. It has everything you need to do an assessment of what you are and help you determine where you want to be and then give you some information on how to get there.

I have written this book for you. Maybe just for you. At least you are the one who is reading it right now. You are here because you need to be here. Either you bought it, or someone gave it to you, or you stole it. The bottom line is, here you are, book in hand, ready to get going. Take advantage of this time with me. Let me rough you up a little bit. Let me tell you the truth as I have discovered it. Let me show you a way to get what you want out of life. You deserve it. So read the book and do what it says.

WARNING: CLICHÉS AHEAD

The truth hurts.

Heard that one before? It's true. Some clichés are really true. In fact, this is one of my favorites and has become the basis by which I measure the truth: If it hurts, it's probably the truth. So if someone tells you something that doesn't bother you at all and makes you feel all warm and fuzzy and sounds just so sweet and too good to be true, you can bet it's a lie.

The truth will set you free.

Another oldie but goodie in the cliché world. In fact, that one is even in the Bible, which for some of you will guarantee that it must be true. But while true, I think it's incomplete. Yes, I have the audacity to think I can improve on a Bible verse. Actually, I am going to let Werner Erhard improve on it:

The truth will set you free, but first it will piss you off.

That's what this book might do to you. In fact, maybe it already has. If that's the case, then good. We are already making progress.

ACKNOWLEDGMENTS

To my wife, Rose Mary, who has put up with more than any person should ever have to put up with in order to learn how to be in a relationship with me. I am not an easy person to live with or be around most of the time—I know that and so does everyone who knows me—but she knows and understands that better than anyone and loves me in spite of it all. She deserves a prize for putting up with me, my eccentricities, my rage, my passions, my energy, my intolerance, my silliness, my boundless ego, my noise, and my stuff. Bless her.

To my boys, Tyler and Patrick. No two siblings could be as different and yet similar in so many ways as well. They have given me a ride on a roller coaster of emotions that I wouldn't trade for anything. I am proud of them in every way and grateful to them for becoming men who are my two best friends.

To my friends, and there aren't many. This includes my speaker buddies and the other few personal friends I have, as well as some other individuals who appeared quite anonymously along the way to guide me when I needed help, and gave me encouragement and chastisement. Each helped me more than I can ever say in their unique and different way.

To Matt Holt of John Wiley & Sons, Inc. Matt was the first guy willing to step out on a limb and publish an edgy, confrontational book that went against the grain of the entire self-help genre. He took a chance on me, an unknown in the publishing world. Look how well it worked out for both of us!

ABOUT THE AUTHOR

Caustic. Irreverent. Edgy. Controversial. Sarcastic. Refreshing. Hilarious. All words used to describe bestselling author and television personality, Larry Winget. Larry is a philosopher of success who is unique in every way. No one says what he says or looks like he looks. He is a true one-of-a-kind in a sea of same ol' same ol'.

Larry is a five-time *New York Times/Wall Street Journal* best-selling author. His books, translated into 14 languages, include *Shut Up, Stop Whining, and Get a Life*; *It's Called Work for a Reason*; *You're Broke Because You Want to Be*; *People Are Idiots and I Can Prove It*; and *Your Kids Are Your Own Fault*. Larry is also a television personality who has hosted his own series on A&E, appeared in national television commercials, been featured in two CNBC specials, and had his own PBS special. He has appeared on many national news shows and appears regularly on Fox News and Fox Business. He is a member of the International Speaker Hall of Fame and is considered a financial/personal development/business/parenting guru to people all over the world. For more information go to www.larrywinget.com and follow him on both Facebook and Twitter.

INTRODUCTION

I'm a simple guy. I have simple ideas. It's true. I believe that everything it takes to become more successful either personally or professionally is simple. Idiot simple, in fact.

Want to lose weight? Eat less—exercise more. Simple.

Want more money? Earn more—spend less. Simple.

Want to be more successful? Stop doing the things that keep you from being successful. Again, simple.

There is nothing complicated about success. We make it complicated. We even want it to be complicated. The reason we want it to be complicated is that believing success is complicated gives us a reason not to be successful—after all, it's complicated! Stop believing all that complicated crap and come over to my side where life is much simpler. Come over to my way of thinking where money is easy, success is simple, and where most every problem you have can be solved with simple solutions.

Before you start to disagree with me about how simple life is, please notice what I am saying. I am using the word *simple*. Never have I used the word *easy*. I don't believe there is anything easy about being successful. Easy is much different than simple.

Is it a simple thing to eat less? Absolutely. Is it easy to do? No. Is it a simple concept to exercise more? Sure! Is it easy to do? Not at all. It's hard to eat less and exercise more. I know! I try to do it every day and it's hard for me to do and I know it's hard for you to do too. But I also know it's simple.

I never kid around when it comes to telling people that success is hard work. I know it is because I have worked hard my whole life. Still do. I do things right now that my buddies of similar stature in the business would never do. I am not too good to work hard. I often do big seminars where I have a staff of people packing and unpacking books and other products and I am right there with them. Lifting, carrying, packing and unpacking, and selling stuff just like they do. Do I have to? No. Then why do I? Because there is work to be done and I'm not too good to do it.

Every aspect of success requires hard work. I once did a big wealth seminar put on by a major seminar company where one of the guys on the program had a booth that displayed the headline, "The QUICK and EASY Way to Become a Millionaire." He was selling a program that cost thousands of dollars and I knew it was all total BS. I knew he was preying on the fears of the crowd in order to take their money. What he was doing certainly wasn't illegal or maybe even unethical or immoral by most people's standards. But what he was doing just wasn't right by my personal standards. I went onstage and told people to be careful of anyone who promises that becoming a millionaire is quick and easy. I know lots of millionaires, and every one of them would agree with me that becoming a millionaire is always slow and hard. I also told them that I knew the other speakers at the conference would sell 10 times more product than I did because they were promising the crowd that they could all become millionaires and I wasn't. The other guys said anyone could become a millionaire and that it wasn't hard at all. Those are lies and I told the crowd that. I knew that few would buy my products because I wasn't going to kiss their butts and promise something that wasn't true. Not just anyone can become a millionaire. Why? Because few will work hard enough to make it happen. I was right; each of these guys sold hundreds of thousands of dollars worth of their products and I sold about a tenth of that. One of the speakers came up to me at the end and said I was pretty rough on the other speakers by saying what I said. I told him I couldn't sleep at night promising people something that I knew they couldn't actually make happen. I told him I was just out to tell people the truth whether anyone liked it or not. He asked me how much I sold and he told me he sold 20 times that much. He was proud. I thought he should have been ashamed. The people who bought my stuff actually got some value and some truth.

That's what I'm going to do throughout this entire book. I promise you that I will never try to sell you an idea that you can't make happen if you are willing to do it and combine it with some hard work. I won't blow smoke up your skirt and tell you that having a positive attitude will fix your problems. I will always tell you my version of the truth. And my version is simple and involves lots and lots of hard work. Did I mention hard work? Again—it's always going to take hard work!

That's why many people don't like what I have to say. Yeah, I know, who could possibly not love every word, right? Believe it or not, it's true. People don't like what I have to say because I promise hard work is the key to changing your life. Hard work is never going to sell like a positive attitude is going to sell, but it will get you a lot farther.

So there you go. A simple guy with simple solutions to all of life's problems and a promise that you have to work your butt off to make it happen. That's what you can expect from me every time. And while this book is full of ideas on how to be more successful, I could summarize my simple principles of success for you with these few lines:

Your life is your own damn fault.
Take responsibility for it.
Learn what you need to do to fix it.
Take action on what you've learned.
Know that hard work on the right things is the key to
    changing your results.
Enjoy the results.

BEFORE YOU START

Don't even think about beginning this book without a highlighter and a pen and paper handy. There's a lot of good stuff in this book, and you're going to want to highlight things to refer to again later. I also encourage you to make notes in the margins and fill in all the forms and to write in the book all you want. It's your book for your private use, and you should use it not only as a reference book but also as a workbook.

If you are going to use quotes from this book either in your own writing or speaking, or if you want to share what I have said in this book with others, then remember: I said this stuff. Give me credit. If I didn't say it, then I have given credit to the person who did. If you quote them, give them credit. If you write a book and I quote you, then I will give you credit. Sound fair? I don't like my stuff stolen any more than you do, so don't steal, just reference it.

Don't share this book. If you think it's good enough that you want your friend to read it, buy her a copy. By the time you finish the book it should be marked up and written in anyway, and that will make it too personal to share with anyone else. Besides, it's just tacky to give someone a used book that has been written in. If you think you are going to loan your book to someone who should read it, and you expect to have it returned, then you are truly naive. (Besides, how am I going to make any money if you give away your book? Buy another one or two or even a case to share with those who need to shut up and stop whining.)

If you don't like the book, then please don't feel compelled to share that with me. I don't care. Seriously, I don't. I am not interested in your criticism or your ideas on what I should have said, could have said, or you wish I had said. I do that enough after I finish writing a book; your criticism won't do me much good and it's too late to change anyway. And don't think I am going to give you a refund just because you don't like the book. That won't happen no matter how much you hate it or how unhappy you are with what I've said, or with me. And if you are going to review the book, read it first. Don't talk about a book you haven't read. If you read it and don't like it, go ahead and say so in your review. But don't go online and talk about the way I dress or my earrings or what you heard someone else say about the book—that isn't fair to me or the people who read your so-called review. By the way, if you do like the book, then say that too in your review, that would be nice. Okay, ready? Let's get this show on the road. . . .

CHAPTER ONE

SHUT UP!

"What? You just told me to shut up?"

Yes, I sure did. Someone needs to. Someone has probably needed to tell you that for a long time. In fact, maybe they already did but you were so busy talking you didn't hear them. If you're like most of the people in the world you are probably talking so much you cannot even hear what is being said. As my dad always told me: "You are broadcasting when you ought to be tuned in." In other words, shut your mouth for a minute and pay attention.

That is most people's biggest problem, including yours. You have been so busy talking and making noise that you never stopped long enough to pay attention to what others were telling you. You probably missed all the important lessons that life was screaming at you because you couldn't hear them.

"Most of us are so busy running around creating the soap opera and drama we call our lives that we don't hear anything."
—Louise Hay

In the New Testament there is a story about Jesus traveling in a fishing boat with his disciples. A big wind comes up, the waves rise, and all of the disciples think they're going to die. They awaken Jesus from his nap, whining and crying, and he says, "Hush, be still" (Mark 4:39 KJV). Then he goes on to talk to them about their faith. (But he first has to make the winds, the waves, and the disciples hush.)

When I was growing up, I was often told to "Hush!" I knew exactly what it meant. In fact, the word "hush" has been shortened to "shhhh." (I bet you didn't know that, did you? See, you are already learning stuff.) When you hear "hush" or "shhhh" you know it means to be quiet. Actually I think if those words of Jesus were being translated today, they could just as easily be, "Shut up! Be quiet! I'm about to teach you something."

And that is exactly what I am saying to you here. Shut up! I am about to teach you something.

SHUT UP AND LISTEN

It's impossible to listen while you are talking. It just can't be done. It's like sneezing with your eyes open: You can't do it. That's why I begin this book with "Shut up." It's so you can finally stop the chatter and listen and learn something. After all, the goal really is to teach you the things you can do to create success in your life, but you are going to have to listen to learn them. You can't learn while you are talking. You can only learn when you are listening. When was the last time you really got quiet and listened? I mean really listened? You should try it some time. You might be amazed at what you hear and even more amazed at what you learn. Jimi Hendrix once said, "Knowledge speaks but wisdom listens."

Listen to Others

Where do you start? I know that's an issue because we live in a noisy place full of people talking. And I will agree that much of what is being said isn't worth listening to. But some of it is. So give this a shot: Listen to your spouse or significant other. I don't mean the kind of listening you do when the TV is blaring in the background or when the kids are screaming in the back seat. I mean the kind of listening when you can be alone, shut out the noise, and really listen and communicate. This special exchange will take you to new heights in your relationship.

Listen to your kids. Parents think that all they do is talk and listen to their kids but the facts prove different. The average parent spends less than three-and-one-half minutes per week in meaningful communication with their children. Which means in a 50-50 give and take, only 90 seconds per week is spent listening. No wonder our kids are such a disaster; we aren't listening to them. You would be amazed at what they would tell you if you would just shut up and listen to them. I know how hard it is to communicate with your kids. I have been there. Especially when you are the parent of a teenager. Sometimes, the last thing your teenager wants to do is talk to you. Usually it's just easier not to talk to them because all they do is make monosyllabic grunts in response to you. Tough. Make them talk. Bug the hell out of them and force the communication if you have to. Both of my sons went through periods when they hated talking to me. How sad for them. I just kept talking and forced them to listen. Then I made them talk and forced myself to listen, even when what they had to say was hard for me to listen to. For instance, one time my son, Tyler, told me I ought to listen to my own speech. Ouch!

Most people think communication is about talking. That is only a small part of it. Listening is the biggest part. Become very good at it with those you love.

Listen to Your Customers

Earl Nightingale said, "All of the money you are ever going to have is currently in the hands of someone else." In business, we call that "someone else" the customer. They have the money. They share it with us when we serve them well. One of the ways you serve your customers well is by listening to them.

You might be saying you don't really have customers, but we all have customers. You might not call them customers, but you still have them. You might call them patients, clients, co-workers, or the audience, but they are still your customers. Listen to them. They have all of the information necessary for you to serve them, solve their problems, and make them happy. Do those things and you will be rewarded.

Listen to Those Who Know More Than You Do

Someone knows more than you do. That may be hard for you to believe but it's true. And some of those who know more than you will happily share that information with you. Folks who have made it are usually more than willing to help others, but they never get asked. The fact is, few ask and even fewer take action when they have been given the answer. How stupid is that? When you ask someone who knows more than you do, take their advice and do what they tell you to do. Remember, they know what to do and have done it, you don't!

By the way, do you want to know a quick way for finding out if someone knows more than you do? Look at their results. Results never lie. If their results are better than yours, then they know something you don't know. Or maybe they are just willing to do more than you are willing to do. In any case, pay attention to that person to determine why their results are better than yours.

Spend some time with those who are doing better than you. Watch them. Listen to them. Figure out what they are doing and then go do it yourself. If you duplicate their effort, then you will duplicate their results. As my friend Joe Charbonneau said, "Do what the masters do and you will become a master."

Listen to the Experts

Great speakers, teachers, philosophers, and other experts have information that is readily available in many formats. Don't think you have to know the great teachers to learn from them. The bookstore, library, and Internet are full of everything you need to know to become more successful in any area of your life.

Listen to Great Music

I love great music. It can take me back in time to when I was a kid, or to a place I enjoyed with my wife, or can transport me to a calm meditative place. It can make me smile, make me cry, make me laugh, and put me to sleep. I use music to entertain myself, to inspire me, and to relax me. You can too.

My personal favorites are Leon Russell, Elvis, Merle Haggard, Willie Nelson, Van Morrison, classic country, and classic rock, but I enjoy about everything. But I will promise you this, just because I'm listening to it, I won't play it so loudly that you will be able to hear it in your car when I'm playing it in mine!

Listen to Your Self

Notice I did not say "yourself." I said "your *Self*." I don't mean you should talk to yourself and listen to it—although you do that all the time. I'm talking about listening to your *Higher Self*. The "better you" that knows what you ought to be doing. You might call it your conscience. You might call it your gut. Some people call that *Higher Self* God, and they might be right. I don't really care what you call it; I just want you to listen to it. It's smarter than you are. It's tuned in at higher levels than you are. It knows! So listen to it. You also might try doing what it says.

Sometimes, You Should Not Listen

"Wait, first you say to listen and now you are telling me not to listen. Make up your mind. So are there really things I should not listen to?"

Yes. Just like there is a list of things and people you should listen to, there is also a list of things and people you should not listen to.

- Do not listen to someone who is broke telling you how to be rich.
- Do not listen to a fat doctor who smokes telling you what it takes to be healthy.
- Do not listen to someone telling you how to be successful when they are not.
- Do not listen to a preacher telling you that you are a worthless sinner.
- Do not listen to people who put other people down.
- Do not listen to office gossip.
- Do not listen to anyone who puts you down for any reason at any time.
- Do not listen to someone who is more interested in selling you than serving you.
- Do not listen to only one side of an argument. Listen to both sides before making up your mind.
- Do not listen to someone with bad results telling you how to get good results.
- Do not listen when someone says, "Do as I say, not as I do."

One more, and this one needs additional explanation. I told you to listen to your *Self*. And you should. But be very careful when you listen to yourself. No one will ever talk as badly about you or to you as you will to yourself. Do your best to control that negative self-talk. When you catch yourself saying things like "I could never do that" or "I'm not good at that" or "I'm so stupid"—STOP! Regroup and restate what you should be saying to yourself: "I can do this!" and other things that move you closer to the result you want, not further from it. Be honest and deal with the facts of your actions and your capabilities when talking to yourself. Don't be negative unless it's true, and then use that truth to take action so you can move to a better place.

"Okay Larry. I get it. Some of this is stuff I already know. In fact, most of this stuff is the same old stuff you promised I wouldn't be hearing. When do we get to the good stuff? What's next?"

Are you ready for the good stuff? I'm almost there. But we have to lay some groundwork first. This is all foundational work. Don't worry. It's about to get ugly.

So what's next? Easy. Stop whining.

CHAPTER TWO

STOP WHINING!

Whining is everywhere. Open your ears and you will hear it in every restaurant, at the supermarket, on television, on Facebook, on Twitter, on the radio, in your workplace, in your home, and even inside your own head or coming out of your own mouth. And people will let you get by with all of it. Why? Whining has become so prevalent, we barely notice anymore. Whining is not the exception; it's our everyday way of life.

The Republicans whine about the Democrats and the Democrats whine about the Republicans. Turn on any of the reality programs (where there is actually little reality) and you will hear one "housewife" whine about the other one or hear one idiot, out of control, spoiled brat teenager whine about the other brainless, hair-gelled, spray-tanned twerp. Whining is at the center of every political debate, nearly every television show, and is the centerpiece of our society.

Whining is the biggest problem we are dealing with today. It's easier to whine about our problems than it is to take action and fix our problems. It's easier to blame someone else for our situation than it is to take responsibility, face our issues, and turn our situation around. It's easier to wallow in our misery than to get over it because wallowing in our problems gets us sympathy from other whiners and feeds our failure; whining never asks us to accept that we are the cause of all of our problems.

Whining makes me sick. What I find is that the whiners, if you can get them to shut up for a minute, are also sick of whining. They are whining to get attention, and they really want someone to grab them and tell them to shut up, stop whining, and get a life!

So if you are a whiner, and we all are from time to time, I believe you are sick of it and are ready for things to change. You are sick of not doing well; sick of the failures; sick of being broke; sick of lousy relationships; sick and tired of being sick and tired; just plain sick of it all. Am I right? Of course I am. Okay, here's your first step in turning it around.

> **If you are unhappy, unsuccessful, sick, or broke—please just keep it to yourself. The rest of us do not want or need to hear about it, so don't feel compelled to share!**

The following letter is a prime example of the kind of whining I am talking about. It's a real letter that was sent to me by a "fan." I have not changed one word of it—not the punctuation, not the grammar, and not the whining.

Dear Mr. Winget,

I hope you can find time in your busy schedule to read my letter. I am so troubled, I truly wish you can help. I will try to make this as brief as possible. I am a thirty-six year old hairstylist. I am single, and my life is so painful. I really do not know who to turn to. My dream in life is to have a successful career doing something I enjoy. But my biggest dream in life is to get married and have a family. And that dream has just been shattered. I met and fell in love with the girl of my dreams. It was heaven sent, we both thought the world of each other. But she decided we were moving too fast and she left me. I am completely devastated and heartbroken. We had both told each other that we were perfect for each other. Now I am alone. My second problem is my career. Throughout my life growing up I was brought up to be a pro baseball player by my parents. They never taught me the importance of school, as long as I could hit homeruns. Well I barely graduated high school. That summer I had tryouts with two professional teams. I did not make either team. Now I was lost. I had to take any job I could. For years I always thought I was going to be a star in the major leagues. I never gave any other career a thought. I decided to become a hairstylist. Schooling was only a year, and I would have a career. I never really had it in my heart to be a hairstylist. Now fifteen years later I am miserable. I do not want to be a hairstylist any more. This depresses me every day. I would love to have a career helping people not end up like me. Help them set goals and help them obtain them. How do I get a career like that? My third problem is that I am in major financial debt. I just recently filed for bankruptcy. I had a major gambling problem, which is now under control. This is so difficult for me I feel so trapped. I want to change careers, settle down and get married. But with my financial problem I cannot do either. Please I would truly appreciate any advice you could share with me. I am heartbroken, broke and confused.

Thank you sincerely,
Joe Bob Whiner (Not his real name but it should be.)

Are you sick yet? Is it any wonder his girlfriend left him? When I read this letter I nearly threw up! Want to know what my advice was? "Shut up, stop whining, and get a life!" I wrote this guy back and told him I had never read such a pitiful pile of drivel in my life. I told him that he was sickening to himself and to everyone around him and now to me; I asked how could he be surprised by his crummy life when his outlook on life was so crummy. Then I went on to explain in detail what was wrong and what he could do to fix his life. I gave him the condensed version of this book (you are getting the whole load). But the message is the same. By the way, about six weeks later the guy wrote me another letter thanking me for being the only person who ever told him to quit whining and get on with his life. The other responses he received were "nice" and commiserated with him about how sad it all was. He said my response had changed his direction and he was making major improvements. However, the really sad thing is that this letter is pretty typical of what is going on in our society.

> **Few people will turn to themselves to take responsibility for their results until they have exhausted all opportunities to blame someone else.**

IT'S EVERYONE'S FAULT BUT MINE

What low have we sunk to when someone writes me defending irresponsible behavior with the words "Personal responsibility is such a cliché. It's a condescending overused phrase that has become the stock answer to everything." Yes! It's the answer to everything! And it's a damn shame that people would rather do anything in this world than take responsibility for their actions, including dismissing the notion as cliché and condescending. We have become a society of victims. "Someone else caused all of the misery I'm going through, it certainly couldn't be my own stupid actions!" We have reached the point where very few are willing to take responsibility for their results. Why should they? No one is really asking them to. Today, you can spend more money than you make, buy more house than you can ever hope to pay for, and there aren't many consequences. In fact, it's the bank's fault you did it in the first place! You can show up for work, steal from your employer, do a crappy job, and not much can be done because chances are your union will protect you from the consequences. You can spill hot coffee in your lap and get a million bucks because you spilled the coffee in your own lap. No one else poured it there. (And if the coffee had not been that hot, you would have gone back and demanded a hotter cup!) You can get drunk in a bar, crawl behind the wheel of your car, have an accident, maybe even kill someone, and sue the bartender for over-serving you. You can complain about how unfair the system is and never be held to any accountability for your "plight."

I am sick of parents blaming the violence on television as the reason their kid just blew up the neighbor's dog or for school shootings. Violence on television and in the movies is too prevalent—I will give you that. And I will also agree that many people are susceptible to what they see or listen to. But lousy parenting is the real cause of messed up kids.

I am sick of listening to people blame their lousy life on the fact they have ADHD, or they were first-born, or they were breast-fed or bottle-fed, or because they have restless leg syndrome.

I am sick of people blaming and then suing cigarette companies because they are dying of cancer. Didn't they know cigarettes are not good for them? Let me see, the concept is that you set something on fire and then you suck that fire down into your lungs. Did they really think that was the purpose of lungs? If they are really that stupid then they deserve their problem.

I am sick and tired of listening to fat people blame their genes for their obesity. Chances are they haven't been able to fit into their jeans for years! People are fat because they eat too much. Period. Only about 1 percent of obesity is caused from thyroid problems or anything genetic. The primary reason people are fat is that they overeat and then they get little or no exercise. It's their own fault. Think about it: Did you ever eat anything by accident? It isn't McDonald's fault you said, "Super-size that for me." None of the fast food places held a gun to your head and forced you to eat their food. You did it. It's your own fault and you are responsible for your fat belly—not them.

Source: Larry Winget, "Shut Up, Stop Whining, and Get a Life," SmarterComics.

I just covered a story during an interview on Fox Business where a woman wanted a refund on three years of tuition because the prospects of her getting a high paying job as an attorney are not as good as when she first went into law school. Sorry things didn't work out as you planned, sweetheart, but welcome to life! There are lots of soldiers who joined the Army and now find themselves in a ditch with bullets flying past their heads, and I'm sure some are saying "Damn! This isn't what I had in mind at all when I joined." But they deal with it. You make a decision in life and sometimes it works out and sometimes it doesn't. There are no money-back guarantees, bail-my-sorry-ass-out, this-isn't-what-I-expected, give-me-another-chance do-overs in life. You *deal* with it. And you don't complain about it because you made the decision in the first place.

STUFF IS GOING TO HAPPEN

When stuff happens to you it just proves you are alive, because as long as you live, stuff is going to happen. Stop thinking you are one of the special ones that nothing happens to. Those people don't exist, and if they did, who would really want to hang around them anyway? They would be so boring. What would they have to talk about? How perfect everything is in their lives? Wouldn't you just want to slap them?

The stuff that happens to you is what makes life interesting—both the good stuff and the bad stuff. It's called life. It isn't perfect. It is just life. Deal with it. Put up with it. Enjoy it as best you can. But please, whatever you do, do not whine about it.

Someone sent me this—it's one of those stupid things that get passed around with no one to give credit to, or I would happily do it. While most of the Internet stuff passed around is pretty much worthless, I liked this one:

IF . . .
If you can start the day without caffeine,
If you can always be cheerful, ignoring aches and pains,
If you can resist complaining and boring people with your troubles,
If you can eat the same food every day and be grateful for it,
If you can understand when your loved ones are too busy to give you any time,
If you can overlook it when those you love take it out on you when, through no fault of yours, something goes wrong,
If you can take criticism and blame without resentment,
If you can resist treating a rich friend better than a poor friend,
If you can face the world without lies and deceit,
If you can conquer tension without medical help,
If you can relax without liquor,
If you can sleep without the aid of drugs,

If you can honestly say that deep in your heart you have no prejudice against creed, color, religion, gender preference, or politics,
Then you have reached the same level of development as your dog.

Life can be complicated and hard at times. Celebrate that. It's what makes us human. And interesting.

"Whoa, Larry, cut me some slack!"

I won't cut you any slack! You earn slack. No one is going to cut you any slack except your momma, so stop asking others to cut you some slack. Why should they? Life doesn't issue Get Out of Jail Free cards for being stupid. Stop expecting the world to rescue you. The Lone Ranger isn't coming. Clean up your own mess. Fix your own problem. Admit you are an idiot and commit to do better next time. Stop fixing the blame and start fixing the problem! Remember this if you don't remember one other thing in this book: Your life is your own fault. You created it. You are responsible. You did it. No one else. And the good news is that you can fix it!

THE REAL DANGER OF WHINING

Whining prolongs the problem. As long as you continue to whine about what is wrong with your life there will be no room for anything good to come into your life. That's just the way life works. You can't focus on the solution when you are whining about the problem. You can't do two things at once. Pick the one that moves you closer to where you want to be in life. Does whining bring you closer to success? Does whining bring you closer to a better relationship? Does whining really make you happy? Does it make you smile? Seriously, have you ever seen anyone smile and whine at the same time?

The answer obviously is that whining does not move you closer to where you want to be. Whining will only make your problem stick around longer. It will not make you happy, it will not bring you peace, and trust me on this one: It will not endear you to others.

What moves you closer to where you want to be and what you want to have? A plan. When you have a plan for dealing with your situation, you are energized. You are happier. You are focused on the solution. That's when your life moves forward. And you can't plan and whine at the same time.

Remember: You can only choose one thing to do, so what's it going to be? Are you going to whine and stay stuck? Or are you going to create a plan that moves you toward the life you want?

I UNDERSTAND PROBLEMS

"But you don't understand, Larry!" Yes, I do. More than you know. People have problems. People get laid off, they get fired, they get downsized, upsized, and rightsized. I understand these things happen. I get hundreds of e-mails each month from people with real problems. Some of the stories are heartbreaking and just aren't fair. I'm aware of all the bad things people are faced with economically and with their health and their kids and everything else that hits people between the eyes every day. And I understand these things happen to really good people who don't deserve them to happen. That's the way life is—bad things do happen to really good people. I am not closing my eyes to these things. I am not saying you caused the economy to go south or your company to be sold. I'm not saying you caused your kid to take meth or that you gave your spouse cancer. Those things are not your fault. But how you react to those things is your fault. And when I say "your fault" I mean you are responsible. And if that makes you uncomfortable or mad, it doesn't really matter; it's still true.

Life does not just happen to you; you happen to life. So you got dealt a crummy hand. It happens. Pick up the cards, shuffle them, and deal yourself a new hand. You are in control. Don't let another minute pass without taking positive action. Don't whine about it. Instead get busy. Good things don't interrupt you. You have to make them happen. And that is what is up next: discovering how to get the life you always wanted.

If you don't have much going wrong in your life, then you don't have much going on in your life.

CHAPTER THREE

GET A LIFE!

Old joke:

A guy goes to the doctor and says, "Doc, it hurts when I do this." And the doctor says, "Then don't do that!"

That's the key to "getting a life." Stop doing the things that hurt you. Simple idea again, huh? The key is identifying what those things are. That's not so hard either. Are you sick of living life in a "less than" way? Having less than you want? Less than you dreamed of? Less than you deserve? Are you finally ready to do something about it? Are you ready to change?

I doubt it.

"What? How can you be so cruel? How can you say you doubt that I am ready to change?"

Easy. I've heard it all before. You have probably said it all before as well.

I start every speech I give with these questions: "How many of you are ready to be more successful in the future than you ever were in the past? How many of you are ready to make more money in the future than you ever did in the past? How many of you are ready to have more fun in the future than you ever did in the past?" I ask them to respond by yelling out "You bet!" at the end of each question. Everyone eagerly does. How many of those people do you think really become more successful, make more money, or have more fun? I doubt if very many of them do. Your response might be that it's because I did not give that great a speech. That certainly could be. But I think there is much more to it than that.

19

READY, WILLING, AND ABLE

Remember the old saying "Ready—Willing—Able"? We have heard that most of our lives. It's one of the most recognizable clichés.

Ready

Here is how I look at that statement: Everyone is ready. Or at least they think they are, or say they are. That is why they all yell "You bet!" at the questions I ask in my speeches. And I actually think when people say they are ready, they are. I honestly have never met anyone who was not ready for more.

Able

Skip to the third item on the list: able. How many are able? Everyone. Seriously. No matter what you face; whether it's a mental, financial, or physical liability, you are still able to do more. Even if it's just a little bit more. And if you do a little bit more, you get a little bit more. But the magic of this action is that when you do a little more sometimes, not always but sometimes, you get a lot more.

So, if everyone really is ready to do better and to have more, and everyone really is able to do more and become more, then what is the problem?

Willing

The answer to that question lies in the second word: willing. Is everyone willing to become more or to do more in order to have what they want in life? The answer is a screaming NO! And that is the problem. People are not willing to put in the hours or put in the effort to change. The world really isn't made up of the "haves" and the "have-nots." It's made up of the "wills" and the "will-nots."

Again, the question is never, "Can someone do better?" Of course they can. And it's never, "Are they able to do better?" Of course they are able. The question is always, "Will they do better?" Sorry, but the truth is, most just won't. Not because they can't and not because they aren't able, but simply because they aren't willing.

See how simple it is? You have probably been asking yourself for a good long time why your life isn't better. Now you have the answer. The answer is that you aren't willing to do what it takes for your life to be better.

"That doesn't sound very fair."

Of course it does. It's perfectly fair. Your life is the way it is because you haven't been willing to do what it takes to make it different. Period. Case closed. Deal with it.

And sadly, it's not that you haven't wanted it to be better. Want has little to do with it. You can desperately want success and never achieve it. You can want to be rich and never make any money. You can want to lose weight and only get fatter. Want only matters if you want enough to be willing to do whatever it takes to achieve the desired result.

> The world really isn't made up of the "haves" and the "have-nots."
> It's made up of the "wills" and the "will-nots."

THREE MORE REASONS PEOPLE AREN'T SUCCESSFUL

I have already told you one of the reasons you aren't successful: You haven't been willing to do what it takes. But since I know people don't like just one reason, I am going to give you three more—three I know you won't like at all!

1. You're stupid.
2. You're lazy.
3. You don't give a damn.

Three Main Reasons People Are Not Successful:
They are stupid.
They are lazy.
They don't give a damn.

Ouch! Still recoiling a bit from that? A little too harsh for you? Too bad. It's still true, and remember: The truth hurts! That's how you know it's the truth.

The common word in each of these reasons is you. You are the reason your life sucks. In other words, if your life sucks it's because you suck. It's not because conditions suck. It's you.

We are all given the same list of things in life to deal with:

- The economy
- Taxes
- Insurance
- Aging
- Stupid people we have to work with
- Kids
- Bills
- Crazy customers
- Not enough time
- Not enough money

Does this list look familiar to you? It should, because all of us are dealing with a list that looks just like it. While we all have pretty much the same list, some people take the list and get rich while other people take the list and go broke. You know what? It isn't the list's fault. It's your fault.

You want to know the truth about why you aren't doing well? Here's one reason: You.

If your life sucks, it's because you suck.

Stop making worthless, flimsy excuses and face the music: You are either stupid, lazy, or you don't give a damn. So which is it? Or is it all three of them?

"Yeah but Larry..." Don't "Yeah but" me. I don't care. I don't want your excuses. Because that's what they would be: excuses. Not reasons, just excuses. There is a big difference. Reasons are real. Excuses are not real. Yes, they exist, but they are not real in the sense that they are keeping you from doing well. They are only excuses that give you a way to keep from accepting responsibility. Excuses allow you to point the finger of blame away from yourself. Reasons force you to point the finger of blame in the direction it should be pointed—in your own face.

I will listen to a reason. I will even try to understand it. I may even do my best to tolerate it. And I will give you a little while to deal with it and overcome it. But excuses? Sorry, no slack when it comes to excuses.

Let me say again that I do understand adverse conditions. All of us go through tough times. However, we can't use tough times as an excuse forever. Enough of that—I already beat you up about that in Chapter 2. I want to more closely examine the three reasons people are not as successful as they want to be.

You Are Stupid

Now that I have said it, I want you to know I have a hard time buying this one. None of us knows everything, even though

I often get accused of thinking I do. And all of us can certainly afford to know more than we already do. In fact, you should be reading and listening and learning more every day. Information has never been more abundant or more easily accessible. Libraries are plentiful; bookstores are on almost every corner and most even serve good coffee; the Internet is available to most and has lots of interesting things to learn (in fact, you can find things on the Internet you don't even want to know). So if you are interested in finding information, there is plenty of it around.

Lack of information, though, isn't the problem. And stupidity isn't really the problem. How many people are really stupid? (Please don't raise your hand here!) I don't believe there are really that many stupid people. People know enough just the way they are to be successful. Really. There isn't a person who doesn't know enough to be successful at something. You may not know enough to be successful at anything or at everything—but you know enough to be successful at something.

The problem isn't that you don't know. The problem is that you don't do what you already know. Read that line again if you need to. You know enough, but you aren't doing much with it. In other words, you aren't really stupid at all. You're just lazy.

You Are Lazy

Here is another popular cliché: Knowledge is power. You have heard this your whole life. Yet this cliché is a lie. In fact, I think this is one of the most unfortunate lies ever perpetrated on society. Knowledge is not power. It's the implementation of knowledge that is power.

> **Knowledge is not power.
> It's the implementation of knowledge that is power.**

It's not what you know that matters, it's what you do with what you know that matters. Knowledge alone won't fix anything. It takes effort. It doesn't always take a lot of effort—but it takes at least some effort.

The good news is that some effort is just about all it takes to do well these days. There are many ways to make a living. You can make a living doing almost anything. In fact, I am going to go out on a limb here and say that no one has to be without a job if they really want one.

I know a person who picks up dog poop for a living. Really. In fact, she used to pick up my dog's poop. She would show up once a week, spend about five minutes scooping doggie poop, and move on to the next house and the next pile of poop. Her slogan: "We're #1 in #2."

Is this a crummy way to make a living? Maybe for you. But this woman loves her job. She drives a brand new truck, spends her time outdoors, which she loves, and gets to say howdy to lots of wonderful dogs, which she also loves.

One day a young man about 20 years old rang my doorbell. He had a bucket that contained a couple of cans of spray paint and some number stencils. He wanted to spray my house numbers on my curb since my old ones had faded over the years. Four numbers with a background—all for only five bucks. Five bucks? I said sure and handed over the five bucks. Two minutes later he had finished. He then walked next door and rang my neighbor's doorbell and the process started all over again. I talked to him while he did my neighbor's curb. He explained that he attended college at the University of Oklahoma and had been painting house numbers on curbs for the past two summers. In about 75 days he makes enough money to pay his tuition and room and board for the whole year—at five bucks a pop.

The point here is that there are plenty of ways to make a living. It just takes a willingness to get off your lazy butt and do something. It seems most people would rather be broke and lazy than work a little and have a pocket full of money. They complain being broke is so terrible and in their mind they are saying, "But at least I won't have to break a sweat." In fact, there are people who complain about not having a job but make little effort to get one. They find it easier to accept unemployment benefits than to go to work. Of course it's *easier*—it just isn't the right thing to do.

Maybe you won't be getting hired for the job of your dreams, but at least you will be doing something and earning a paycheck. You will have your dignity and some self-respect. Many companies will hire you with no training and no experience and no skills and then train you. Good news! You can be stupid and still get hired.

Plus, there are plenty of educational programs that are either free or cost very little to attend and that will give you specialized skills so you can land a really good paying job. There are books that will teach you everything there is to know about a given subject. Most of the time, it's not for lack of information that you aren't doing well—it's for lack of effort. It doesn't take a lot of effort to read a book, does it? In fact, you can sit on your lazy butt and do that. But will you? I hope so, but the reality of the situation is that most won't.

You Don't Give a Damn

This is the really ugly reason. This is the one that will paralyze you and keep you broke, unhappy, and unsuccessful.

I will cut you a little slack if you are truly stupid—at least for a while. But you don't get any slack if you are lazy. If you don't care enough to be more and do better, I won't be able to stand being in your presence. If you don't care enough to even try, the knowledge that you even exist will bother me. "Ooh, that's mean." Yep, and I hope it makes you mad enough to give a damn!

Not giving a damn, or not caring, is the ultimate insult to yourself and to your family. To know how to be successful and not care enough to do it's truly a pitiful thing.

How can you look your family in the eye and admit to them you are able to provide a better life for them but won't because you don't love them enough to read a book, take a class, get up a little earlier, turn off the TV a little quicker, or work a little harder or longer?

"Not fair!" you say. Oh, sure it is. If you are mentally and physically able to be better than you are, and to do better than you do, and you don't do it—the only reason I can come up with is that you don't care enough about yourself and your family to do so. Sorry, but that makes me sick.

Let's cut to the chase here. Stop right now and admit you could do more than you are doing. And I don't really care how much you are doing—you could do a little more. Right?

And because you bought this book, you have probably decided you are ready to do more. And maybe you just need someone to show you the way. Hello, my name is Larry Winget, glad I showed up. Let's get started.

TIME TO GET STARTED

Hopefully you are ready. By this time you have stopped your whining, put away all of your excuses, and are ready to create the life of your dreams. But before you do that you need to spend a little time actually designing that life. You can't just run after what you want until you really know exactly what you want.

"But I do know what I want. I want more!"

Okay, here is a dollar. Now you have more. If I gave you a dollar you would have more, right? But that isn't what you had in mind, is it? I know it isn't. But it's still what you said. You have to be more specific than "more."

In the next few pages I am going to help you specifically design the life you want and teach you how to create it.

Get ready—this is going to be fun!

CHAPTER FOUR

LIVE BY DESIGN, NOT BY DEFAULT

Source: Larry Winget, "Shut Up, Stop Whining, and Get a Life," SmarterComics.

You don't get what you want out of life until you know what you want out of life. Otherwise you get what is left over after you spend all of your time living the life someone else has planned for you. You are surviving on leftovers. I hate leftovers. I want to create something new and perfect just for me.

Most people spend more time planning their weekend than planning their life. They don't think past the end of their nose, as my Mom always said. They look at their lives and have no idea how they got in the mess they are in. If that's you, know this: You have created everything that has happened in your life, both the good and the bad. I had a complete business failure and both a business and personal bankruptcy that were my own fault. I created those things. I created every single problem I ever had. I also created my business success and the happiness I am experiencing now. You created your situation, too. It was easy. All you and I did was think, speak, and do.

It's your thoughts, words, and actions that will either move you closer to where you want to be or further away from where you want to be. Those three things are the keys to creating the life you want and have been the keys to the life you are currently living.

You never really have a money problem, a relationship problem, a business problem, or a health problem. You only have a problem with your thinking, your words, and your actions. And when you straighten out your thoughts, words, and actions, everything will begin to turn around for you.

Thoughts are creative. Words are creative. Actions are creative. These are the three creative forces of the universe. Master these and the world belongs to you.

CHANGE YOUR THOUGHTS

Tag Yourself a Winner

Several years ago I got a personalized license plate for my car that said WINNER. I had no idea at the time the kind of impact that tag would have on my life. I found out that when I put a tag on my car that said WINNER, I could no longer drive the way I had been driving. When your tag says WINNER, you can't pull out in front of people and cut them off (not that I would ever do that)! And why not? Would a winner do that? No, only a loser would do that. Would a winner honk at people who cut them off, or who pull away too slowly from a red light? No, a winner would never do that, only a loser would. (Kind of like having a guy with a "Honk if you love Jesus" bumper sticker flip you off.) Would a winner drive a dirty car? Sorry, only a loser would drive a dirty car. I had tagged myself a winner and suddenly my actions had to change in order to back up what I was saying about myself. I became more of a winner in life simply because I had stated to all who saw me that I was a winner.

Call yourself something and you will move closer toward it. Call yourself a winner and you become more of a winner. Call yourself broke, stupid, unable—live a life full of can'ts, won'ts, should have's, would have's, I wish I had's, and if only's—and see what you become. I bet you won't be happy with the results.

Tattooed for Life

My wife and I were sitting in a bar one evening having a cocktail when a young woman (about 30, but still a young woman at this point in my life) struck up a conversation with us. She said she bet I rode a motorcycle. I asked her how she could tell and she said I just had the look: shaved head, goatee, boots, and sunglasses. She then added that she bet I had some tattoos as well. I confirmed that I indeed have several.

She proudly told us she also had one and proceeded to show us her tattoo, which was a broken heart. She was so proud of it. I asked her why she would tattoo a broken heart on her hip. She said she just thought it was pretty. I asked her why she would want to proclaim to the world and to every man she met and even to herself that she had a broken heart? I went on to ask her how her love life was going. She said it sucked; she couldn't keep a boyfriend, and every man in her life treated her horribly.

I asked her when that trend started. She replied that it had all started about five years earlier. I then asked how long she'd had the tattoo of the broken heart, and she said about five years. I then asked if she could see any correlation between the two events. A light came on in her eyes and she said, "You don't think the tattoo is causing my love life to be bad, do you?" My wife, Rose Mary, and I both assured her that indeed we did. She asked what she should do and we told her she should get that tattoo filled in as soon as possible. That way she would be proclaiming to the world and to every man she dated—and to herself—that her heart was whole and full. She said thanks, gave us both a hug, and left immediately to go to the tattoo parlor. Did it work? Who knows? I never saw her again but I'm betting it made a difference. Not to the men she dated, maybe, or to anyone else in the whole world, but it made a difference to the way she thought about herself.

The lesson? Be careful what you proclaim to the world to be true about yourself, whether it be through your words, your actions, or your tattoo. Even the little things can have a big impact.

CHANGE YOUR WORDS

Think again of what the best version of yourself would be. When picturing the best version of yourself stop and ask, "Are the words I use in alignment with the best I can possibly be?" If not, then change the way you are talking.

Saying things like, "I have never been able to do that well" will only perpetuate the fact you won't ever be able to do it well. Saying "I'm not good at math" doesn't make you better at math. Saying "Food always goes straight to my thighs" means you are going to have fat thighs as a result of your eating. "I always get a cold this time of year" is the surest way I know of to catch a cold.

What you say about yourself and your expectations helps to program what happens. Your words attract to you either the life you want, or the life you don't want.

When I was in the telecommunications business, it got to the point I hated going to work. I had the "Sunday Night Blues." Every Sunday night I would just get a bad feeling knowing the next morning I had to get up and go to an office and do something I did not like doing any longer. One day I told my wife, "I'd give *anything* to not have to do this anymore." Well, the universe heard me and I started to create that result into my life. The problem was that the universe did not hear me very clearly. It thought I had said that I would give *everything* not to have to do this anymore. So that is what ended up happening to me. I ended up giving everything I had, and then no longer had to go to work there any longer. I lost it all—my job, my company, my money, my cars, everything. Be careful what you say. It happens.

Instead of saying what you don't want to have happen, begin today proclaiming what you do want to happen. Start with the affirmation I am giving you here. Then go on to create your own personalized version.

This Day

This day, I thankfully accept all of the good things that are coming my way. This day is full of excitement, love, energy, health, and prosperity. This day, people are calling on me to be of service to them and I respond by giving my very best. This day, I think and practice health in my life, refusing to accept anything less than perfect health. This day, I accept the abundance and prosperity that is mine and willingly share it with others. This day, I focus on the moment and give no thought to the past or to the future. This day, I spend in total enjoyment of what I do. This day, I fill with loving thoughts and actions toward all other people and myself. This day, I spend in grateful appreciation of all that is mine. This day, I take action to make sure that I am moving in the right direction. This day, this hour, this minute, this moment is all that I have and I choose to use it in celebration!

I have personally used this affirmation for many years. I read it to myself almost daily. If this affirmation doesn't fit your style, then write your own. Say the things you need to hear to help create the life you want.

Affirmations are powerful. However, don't think that affirmations alone are going to change things for you. Just saying something won't change your results.

Affirmation without implementation is self-delusion.

CHANGE YOUR ACTIONS

Your actions determine what you have. Yet your thoughts and words pretty much determine how you act. If you don't have confidence, you won't act with confidence. If you talk negatively about yourself, then it's going to be hard to act positively. So do just what I've said here about getting your thoughts and words right because they will have a big impact on how you act. But don't doubt this, it still takes action. At some point, it doesn't matter how you think or how you talk, you still have to get things done. You are rewarded for effort . . . for work . . . for action. And a lack of action will leave you just sitting in the dust, broke, unhappy, lonely, with nothing to be proud of except your stubbornness for not doing what you knew you were capable of but were too lazy to do.

Thoughts. Words. Actions. Those three things must change if you want to change your life. But the most important thing is action regardless of what any of the other motivational gurus (bozos) tell you. Don't let them fool you with their words or their promises. They will say that you can "manifest" what you want. What does that even mean? You don't manifest anything. You create your results based on the actions you have taken or not taken. Manifestation is a trick word that we love to hear and use because it doesn't imply any effort is necessary. Don't be fooled by these idiots. And yes, I know most of these idiots personally and think they should be ashamed for selling you these lies. And you should be just as ashamed for believing them. Wake up and use some common sense!

That's the whole problem with the Law of Attraction movement and the book, *The Secret*, by Rhonda Byrne.

THE SECRET IS A TOTAL LOAD OF CRAP

The Secret is without a doubt the biggest load of crap ever put on paper. People love it and have made it one of the bestselling books on the planet, but that doesn't mean it's the truth. The reason people love it is because the whole concept behind it is that you can achieve the results you have always dreamed of simply by focusing on what you want. I get that. In fact, I myself have said a lot about focusing on what you want here. But I won't sugarcoat the reality that focus alone isn't enough to get you the results you want. Besides, most people can't turn off the television long enough to focus on their health, their work, their finances, or their own kids. Focus isn't most people's strong suit. So focus isn't enough.

The Secret basically says, "What you think about and talk about comes about." Okay, that is basically what I have said in the previous few pages myself. However, that's where *The Secret* and

The Law of Attraction people stop and I don't. Because I don't believe, "What you think about and talk about comes about." I believe:

> **What you think about, talk about, and get off your ass and DO something about is what comes about.**

Thinking is important, as I have explained. You must change your thinking in order to change your life. Just as talking is important to changing your life. You must think and speak of yourself and your life and what you want to have happen just as I have laid out. But the old "Change your thinking, change your life" isn't enough anymore. It never was and has done those who bought into it wholeheartedly a huge disservice because it doesn't go far enough. To stop at that would be a half-truth. And a half-truth is a half-lie, and since there is no such thing as a half-lie, it's a lie! That's my issue with The Law of Attraction and *The Secret*: they cheat people of the real gratification and success that comes from having put forth good old-fashioned hard work.

That is why some people like to argue with me about my approach to success. It isn't as warm and fuzzy and full of cute platitudes and promises as other people's approaches. My approach is deeply rooted in the most vulgar, obscene, nasty, four-letter word in our vocabulary: W-O-R-K. That is where it falls apart for most people because they don't want to work. They want to think their way to success. Or they want to talk about all of the success they don't have or the success they will someday have. They actually just want to sit on their butts with their big ol' positive attitude and have success find them. They want to "attract" success by just thinking and talking about it. There are many goofballs telling you that you can attract success at their seminars and on the

Internet, yet from what I can tell, the only people making any money with this idea are those who are selling it.

They also love to talk about increasing your deservability. Which translates to me into increasing your sense of entitlement. You are not entitled to a damn thing. You are rewarded for your efforts. No effort = no reward.

Remember that old Biblical saying, "You reap what you sow"? Most people aren't reaping much because they haven't done any sowing. I grew up in the country where we ate what we raised, and trust me when I say that "sowing" is work. Even reaping is work. But the reaping is the payoff for the work you put out there in the first place. Sadly, many people today are expecting to reap when they didn't bother to sow a damn thing. It doesn't work that way.

The whole thing reminds me of that old saying, "The harder I work, the luckier I get." I know that is how I have always attracted my own success: through hard work.

I have achieved a fair amount of success in my life. And some people are quick to tell me how lucky I am. Well, I guess so. But it sure seems to me that I worked my butt off every day to get so lucky. I stayed up lots of nights plotting and planning and figuring out what action I could take next to make my "luck" happen for me. I scrimped and saved and did without and worked at extra jobs to find that big helping of luck.

I even have buddies in the speaking and writing world who like to point out how lucky I have been in this business. They don't want to know how I put every penny I made back into the business for many years, not taking a dime of it for myself so I could build a business that actually had some value. For the first seven years I did this for a living, my employees made more money than I did just so I would someday have a real business with a product line and inventory and offices and all of the stuff it takes to make a business successful. They don't consider the fact that I packed my own boxes of books and DVDs and CDs and took them myself to the UPS store and shipped them to my various speaking engagements. Not my staff, me. When on the road, no one carries my bags and no limos pick me up. And when the flight gets canceled, I get in a rental car and drive all night if I have to get to the engagement simply because I said I would be there. I do whatever it takes. Yeah, I make a lot of money for what I do. But you won't ever find me talking about how lucky I have been or how I attracted my success. I worked my butt off to be this lucky. And you won't hear me giving credit to some secret. My secret is work. Always has been. I think right. I talk right. But I take action and work on it every day. That's what you are going to have to do as well.

Am I bragging? Maybe. In fact, yes I am. I am proud of what I have accomplished. I am grateful for everything I have but I don't fool myself or anyone else about how I got it. I worked for it.

I deal with people all of the time who are waiting for success to come up and knock on their door with a big fat check instead of going out and creating their own success. I get e-mails from people who have lost their jobs and piss and moan about their employer and how unfair it was and on and on and on. Quick question: Will all of that pissing and moaning put food on the table or pay your bills or take care of your family? No? Then get over it and do something (anything) that will.

So what has this little rant been about?

BUT HOW DO I CHANGE?

Everyone always wants to know how to change, and I am about to tell you. And I promise you won't like the answer. You just change. See? I told you that you wouldn't like it. You wanted a complicated answer. A long, drawn-out process with steps you could tick off as you accomplished them. Sorry. It isn't like that. To change, you just change.

Remember how you did things yesterday? Don't do them that way today. Don't think the way you did yesterday. Don't talk the way you did yesterday. Don't act the way you did yesterday. Today, do it differently.

Got it? It's not as hard as you might think. Some say start small and build up, and change the little things first. Wrong! Change the way you think, the way you talk, the people you hang around with, the places you go, the things you read, the food you eat, the television you watch. Change all of it. The big stuff and the little stuff. Would you tell an alcoholic to become sober by giving up one drink a day? Or a crack addict to wean themselves off? No. You go cold turkey. You change it all. If I were broke, unhappy, and unsuccessful, I would be willing to change the way I brush my teeth if I thought it might make a difference. Remember that the stuff you do now has determined the results you have now. If you don't like those results, then change what you are doing right now.

STOP TRYING

I have probably just about convinced you to get started. Maybe. You are about to say, "Okay, Larry, I'll try." Well then, forget it. Seriously, just forget it. Don't even start if you are only going to try. I hate the word *try*. Yoda, the little green Jedi philosopher from Star Wars, was right when he said, "There is no try. There is only do or do not do."

When someone tells you they will try to come to your party, do you really expect them to show up? I doubt that you do. When you tell someone you are going to try to go to their party, do you really plan on going? I don't think so.

Try is a word you use when you don't have the *cajones* to tell the truth. We should all just be honest. You ask me, "Are you going to come to my party?" I answer with, "No. I don't want to come to your party. I would rather gouge out my eye with a carrot stick than come to your stupid, boring, lame party!" That is honesty!

But none of us would ever do that, would we? Of course not. It's just easier to say, "I'll try." Mostly try is an excuse to yourself. It gives you a way out. "Yes, I will do it" is a commitment. You can be held to a commitment. You can't really hold someone to a try because when they don't do it, they can always offer you their patented cop-out of, "Oh well, I tried."

My advice is to stop trying and stop saying you will try. Instead just do it or don't do it. How do you try to do anything anyway? Stop right now and try to pick up a pencil or pen or whatever is lying next to you. Really, just try to do it. You can't. There is no way to try to pick something up. You either pick it up or you don't pick it up. Period. There is no in-between. Try is an excuse not to do. Give it up. By the way, I am having a party soon. Please try to come!

NOTHING IS NEUTRAL

Everything you think, everything you say, and everything you do matters. It all moves you one direction or the other. Every little "I can't do this" moves you further away from your goal. Every conversation, as meaningless as it may seem to you, means a lot when it comes to achieving what you want.

"So when I am talking to my friends or my co-workers in the hall, you are saying that idle chit-chat has an impact on me getting rich, or healthy, or successful, or happy?"

Exactly. Every word matters. If your conversations are full of complaining or putting people down, and you focus on what you lack, then those conversations are killing your chances for success.

The same applies to every action you take. Sitting through one more television show instead of playing with your kids or having a conversation with your spouse or partner may not seem like a big deal at the time—but it matters.

Sleeping another 30 minutes instead of getting up and exercising matters. Not calling your customer back at the agreed time matters. Showing up 15 minutes late matters.

"Oh come on! This is little stuff. You can't be serious. This stuff doesn't matter—I have been doing stuff just like this for years and nothing bad has happened."

Has anything amazing happened? When you stop letting things slide and start taking advantage of every moment, then amazing things happen. The little stuff matters the most. Everyone gets the big stuff. Very few take care of the little stuff. That is why very few end up rich, successful, happy, and healthy, with great relationships. They take care of the big things and let the little things slide. That's a surefire way to live a life of mediocrity. Not much bad—but not much amazing either.

DESIGN YOUR LIFE

Following is a questionnaire that will help you determine exactly what you want out of life. Take the time right now to fill it out. Don't rush. Take your time and give it some thought. We aren't in any hurry here. Be very specific in your answers—remember this is your life you are creating.

What would I like to accomplish before I die?
What do I want to own that I don't currently own?
What kind of car do I really want to drive?
What kind of house do I want to live in?
At which stores do I really want to shop?
What kind of clothes would I like to wear?

What kind of jewelry would I like to wear?
Which restaurants do I want to go to?
Where would I like to travel?
How would I like to spend my recreational time?
Which people would I like to spend more time with?
What would I really like to do if time and money were not issues?
How much would I like to weigh?
How much money would I like to earn each year?
How much money would I like to have saved/invested?
How much money would I like to give away each year?
What kind of relationship do I want with my spouse/ significant other/partner/lover/special friend?
. . . with my children?
. . . with my family?
. . . with my co-workers?
. . . with my friends?
Summarize your perfect life in the next few lines:

_____

_____

_____

_____

_____

_____

How did you do? Does the life you just designed look significantly different from your current life? I bet it does. Now it's time for some honesty. It's time to look at what you are currently doing to make this life happen. Here is another list for you to work on. It's a list of things you are actually doing to make the life you want to come about. If you don't know where to start, you can answer number one with "I am reading this book and filling out these forms." There. You have the first one. Now keep going.

What am I doing to make this happen?
1. _____
2. _____
3. _____
4. _____
5. _____
6. _____
7. _____
8. _____
9. _____
10. _____
11. _____
12. _____
13. _____
14. _____
15. _____

Okay, that is what you say you are doing. And I will bet you the price of this book you did not get to 15. Very few people are actually doing even 15 things to create the life they want to live.

And I even gave you the first one! Now let me give you another shot at telling yourself the truth.

What am I *really* doing to create the life I want?

1. _____

2. _____

3. _____

4. _____

5. _____

There you go. Did you do better this time? Did you come up with five things you are really doing? I hope so. Soon you will be able to fill the first list too. As you start creating the life you want with just a few action steps, you will find that things get easier for you. You will start to focus more and more on creating the life you want until you reach the point where you are obsessed with living the life most only dream of. You will actually find yourself becoming the list you made. You will look in the mirror and see yourself in the clothes you want to wear, with the jewelry you want to wear, weighing what you want to weigh. You will go to your garage and get in the car you want to drive and go to the restaurant where you really want to go. You will enjoy your relationships and have plenty of time to relax and enjoy your life. In other words, you will be creating the life you want.

YOU GET BY GIVING UP

A word of caution: The life you want comes at a price. Everything comes at a price. Nothing is free. No matter what it is in life you choose, there will be a price tag attached.

Want to be fit, trim, and healthy? The price tag is decreased calories and increased exercise. In other words, you don't *get* fit, trim, and healthy. You *give up* the things that are making you fat.

Want to be rich? You either have to work harder, longer, or smarter—probably all three. You don't just *get* rich. You have to *give up* the things that are keeping you broke.

Want to be successful? You don't *get* success, you *give up* what's making you unsuccessful. The price tag for success is pretty expensive, as you are about to find out.

Want to be happy? Then you have to *give up* everything that makes you unhappy.

And what if you don't want anything? That comes at a price, too. The price is usually poverty, sickness, boredom, apathy, mediocrity, bad relationships, and on and on and on.

The reality of life is that you will pay a price, one way or the other. One price gives you exactly what you want. The other gives you exactly what you don't want. Either way, you have paid the price.

The good news is that the life you want comes cheaper than the life you don't want. The life you don't want makes you miserable, unhealthy, and broke. To me, that is too big a price to pay. It's cheaper to be happy, healthy, and rich. However, only you can choose what to pay.

CHAPTER FIVE

SLAUGHTERING THE SACRED SELF-HELP COWS

You have just spent some time thinking about the life you want. Hopefully you now have a picture of the kind of life you want to lead. You even wrote it down—probably for the very first time in your life. You say you are willing to pay the price. Congratulate yourself! You are now further along than almost any other person on the planet. Very few people have ever made it as far as you just have.

So let's get real about making the life you have designed really happen for you. Let's look at all the areas of life each of us deals with and discover how to move through them and past them to actually get the life you want.

This is where you probably think I am going to address all of the typical self-help stuff like setting and achieving goals, being positive, and that sort of motivational mumbo-jumbo. No. I'm going to give you stuff that is much different than what you have come across before. In fact, I am going to attack most of what you have heard and read and learned.

Some won't like my approach here, but as you have probably figured out by now, I don't care. What you think of me isn't as important as what you become.

And some will think I'm not telling the truth because it's so contrary to what we have been bombarded with for so long, but that doesn't make it untrue. It just makes it unconventional, which, in my opinion, makes it refreshing and worth looking at.

"All great truth begins as blasphemy."

—George Bernard Shaw

YOU HAVE BEEN LIED TO!

Does this really surprise you? At this point in your life do you actually still believe that people are telling you the truth? Please! Business writers and success gurus are not telling you the truth about what it really takes to be successful. They don't care whether you are successful or not. They want to sell books and will say what it takes to do it—even when what they are saying makes no sense at all.

Just because a guy can write a bestseller about business doesn't mean he really knows about business. It just means a lot of copies of the book were sold. It says more about the buyers than it does about the writer. Remember, *Jersey Shore* and *Housewives of "Who Gives a Crap"* are still some of the most watched television shows on the planet. That doesn't mean it's quality programming; it just means a lot of people watch the show.

I'm a professional speaker and have written five national bestsellers myself. I am a member of the Speaker Hall of Fame. I am hired by some of the largest, most respected companies in the world to rant on stage about business and personal success. I attend huge conventions of national associations and do my stuff. I personally know many of the most successful speakers and writers in the country, and I also currently read about one business book every week—all the top sellers. So I actually have some expertise is this area. I know what's being said and I know what people are buying.

Know what? Many of these success gurus are selling you a big ol' bucket of doo-doo. Yep, they are lying to you. I like most of these guys but I also know the truth about most of them. Very few of them actually do what they are telling you to do. They talk the talk, but they don't walk the walk.

I know many of the world's leading customer service speakers and writers. Call them. You will be lucky to get your call returned.

I know many of the leading experts on leadership. Most of them can't keep employees working for them because they are such lousy leaders.

I know most of the world's leading sales gurus personally—the men and women who give the speeches and write the bestselling books. Many can't sell their own sales training.

I know more motivational experts and success teachers than I can count. Not really—I can count pretty high. But let me tell you, most of these guys are anything but successful.

The relationship experts aren't usually in a relationship. The humorists aren't funny. The financial experts are broke. I even know experts on ethics and integrity who don't pay their bills.

These people clearly are not experts. They may be well known and they may have given lots of speeches and sold lots of books, but they aren't true experts. Not in a practical sense. Yet people are clamoring to buy their books and hear their speeches. Again, it says more about the buyer than the seller. People are hungry for the truth. Eager to find the next new thing. So people end up buying these books with the hope of finding something new, some secret that will help them discover what it takes to be successful in business and in life. And while some of those books and speeches have actually helped people, for the most part the information is worthless.

"So, Larry, are you an expert? How do we know you are telling us the truth? Aren't you just trying to sell us a book, too?"

Am I an expert? Absolutely! However, I am not an expert at leadership, though I have led many successful organizations. I have led some into stardom and one into bankruptcy. Which did I learn the most from? The one I led into bankruptcy. I am not an expert at customer service. I have delivered both kinds of service: great and sucky. And I recognize it when I get both, too! I am not an expert at selling, though I have been an award winning salesperson. I am not an expert at money or financial success, though I have gone from bankruptcy to multi-millionaire. I am certainly not an expert at relationships. I have screwed up many of them.

All I am really an expert at is being stupid and learning from it. In fact, I could be the poster child for stupidity. The key is that I learn from my stupidity. I pay attention to my mistakes. I have become an expert at not making the same mistake twice, and learning from every stupid thing I have ever done. And I have become pretty good at communicating it. I am not pretending to be something I am not, and I am not saying I am better than any of the others who write the books and give the speeches. I do more wrong before noon than most people will screw up in a week. But I learn from every stupid mistake I make. And I do my best to be up front about it all.

And of course I want to sell you a book. Hopefully, lots of books. I am a businessman. I do this to make money. I wrote this book to make money. Everything I do is to make money. I don't do this out of some overwhelming need to change the world or to change people's lives. The world doesn't want to change or it already would have changed all on its own and without any help from me. People change their lives when they want to, not because I want them to. No book ever changed a life and no speaker ever did, either. People have the power to change their own lives and no author or speaker should take the credit for it. That statement alone should answer your second question: Am I telling you the truth?

In fact, I am totally addicted to the truth. The cold, hard, ugly, like-it-or-not truth! At least the truth as I see it. That's all any of us can really do: tell the truth as we see it from our own experience, our personal perspective, and in our own style. So I will tell you the truth about all of this motivational mumbo jumbo that is floating around . . . my truth.

ATTITUDE AND MOTIVATION

Source: Larry Winget, "Shut Up, Stop Whining, and Get a Life," SmarterComics.

Let me begin with two things I am absolutely positive of: Attitude isn't everything and motivation doesn't work.

"What? How can you say that? You lie! You are a bad man! I buy books by motivational speakers all the time! I listen to motivational speakers whenever I get a chance. I regularly attend motivational podcasts and I am a friend and fan of every motivational guru on Facebook! So what do you mean attitude isn't everything and motivation doesn't work?"

Well, let me prove it to you. If you are the kind of person you say you are, listening to motivational speakers and reading motivational self-help books, then answer these questions: How is your life? Are you rich, happy, healthy, and successful? No? Well there you go, that stuff doesn't really work, does it? (By the way, if you really are rich, happy, healthy, and successful, then congratulations. But I promise you motivation isn't what got you there.)

Don't you just hate that? You are caught. Don't feel bad. I used to be just like you. I have read literally thousands of motivational, self-help books. I have also listened to at least that many motivational, self-help audios and watched hundreds of videos. I have been to lots of meetings and heard the high-powered, high-priced motivational gurus (some of whom are now my good friends) say all those things about feeling good about yourself and how you have to be positive every waking moment. I have listened to them tell the masses to just have a good attitude and anything will be possible. I would sit on the edge of my seat and eat it up until I would nearly swoon with the idea that if only I had the right attitude, my life would be okay.

Listen, I have had a good, positive attitude all my life and I have had more crap happen to me than you can imagine! I had a great attitude and went bankrupt. I had a great attitude the whole time I had problems in my business, my marriage, with my money, and my health. That wonderful, positive attitude of mine didn't keep one thing from happening to me.

So regardless of what any of the books, tapes, and speakers say, attitude isn't everything. I know that is a lot to swallow since it flies in the face of what everyone else says and everything you have ever heard. Like you, I have seen books out there telling you attitude is everything. You can find coasters and T-shirts and even buy a cute little rock to use as a paperweight that says, "Attitude is Everything." You can even get little coins to carry in your pocket to remind you of the same sentiment. You can buy posters to line your walls. It makes the suckers feel better and lines the pockets of the manufacturers. And it's still a lie because attitude isn't everything!

Attitude Is Important, However . . .

Attitude is important; I will give you that. But it won't keep anything from happening to you. It will help you deal with what happens to you, but it won't keep anything from happening to you. So while it's important, it certainly isn't everything. Attitude is only one thing.

What people sometimes think is if they get their attitude right then they will have no problems, they will have nothing bad happen to them, and they won't even have to work—simply because their attitude is so good.

Attitude alone won't change things. Effort changes things. Thoughts change things. Words change things. Again, remember this: It's what you think about, talk about, and do something about that comes about. That is what changes things: the combination of those three things. It isn't what you have a positive attitude about!

It takes more than being positive, because you can be positively lazy. You can be positively wrong. You can be positively stupid. You can be positively incompetent.

It's not about being positive or negative; it's about what works and what doesn't work. It's about what moves you from where you are to someplace else. It's about what makes things better for you.

It's like those people who ask that old, stupid question: Is the glass half empty or half full? My answer? Who the hell cares? What difference does it make if the glass is half full or half empty? Here is the real issue. Does it quench your thirst? That's what matters. Attitude alone won't quench your thirst. It won't move you from where you are to someplace else. That is why I am not a motivational speaker. Instead I call myself The World's Only Irritational Speaker®. I'm just not sure I can motivate you to move from where you are to someplace else. However, I'm very confident I can make you so irritated with where you are that you will do anything you can to be someplace else.

In order to make positive changes in your life, you first have to get negative about your life.

Get Negative to Get Ahead

You read it right: Get negative! I am so tired of listening to the motivational idiots and the self-help bozos and all of the metaphysical new-agers talk about the power of a positive attitude that I could puke! Just put on those rose-colored glasses, dust off the smiley-face button, plaster that big fake smile on your face, and get after it and you will be happy, healthy, and successful. Really? How's that worked for you so far?

"Whatever the mind can conceive and believe, it can achieve!" Thank you, Napoleon Hill. What if the mind can't conceive anything and you believe you are an idiot? What are you going to achieve then? Around January the first of every year, people start talking about their resolutions and saying, "If I can believe it, I can achieve it!" Which is another favorite line of the positively handicapped, and in my opinion, the positively disillusioned!

Here is the way to make real positive change in your life: get negative! Yep, get negative. Take a realistic look at your life. Slip off the rose-colored glasses and instead use a magnifying glass. Look closely at your results. Recognize and own up to the fact that it was your actions that produced those results. If your results are bad, then your actions were bad. If your results really sucked, then the actions that created those results really sucked. At that point, get negative. Go through every stupid thing you have done. Identify each stupid thought, every stupid action, and feel horrible about every asinine result. Cry about it—tie some emotion to your stupidity! Get so negative about how stupid you have been that you make yourself sick.

Those who will tell you to ignore the bad and instead only reinforce the good are idiots. What if there isn't enough good to focus on? And how will ignoring the bad help rid yourself of the bad? It won't.

Find the bad. Recognize every stupid thing you have done. Get so negative about it that you refuse to continue living that way, choosing that way, and accepting those bad results. Then, make the effort it's going to take to change. That's right—get negative, then get the hell over it! It's time to take action.

Getting negative and then taking action is what will produce positive results. The challenge we all have is that our results are not quite bad enough to cause us to change. If you are facing foreclosure, or bankruptcy, or just got laid off, or been diagnosed with diabetes, then you might be at that point. However, most people are just coasting along, bumping their heads now and again and hoping that things won't get any worse. As long as things aren't really all that bad and their back isn't against a wall, then they won't actually have to take drastic action. These folks are numb to their true situation. Wake up!

Take stock of where you are right now. Look at every area of your life and figure out where you are financially, with your health, your weight, your relationships, and with your career. Hold up a magnifying glass and do some close examination to figure out the actions you have been taking to give you the results you are living with. If the results are good in one area, then give yourself a pat on the back and keep on doing what you've been doing. But if the results are bad in another area, take a closer look and then get negative. Know you deserve more and can do better. Refuse to accept the same results in the future. Vow to change things (your results) by changing your actions. Know that you can do it *if* it's important enough for you to do it.

Positive change comes from first recognizing what you have done that you aren't happy with and then getting negative enough to fix it.

ATTITUDE IS ONLY PART OF THE SOLUTION

Work: that dirty word I have already spoken of. You are paid for effort—the effort to serve others well. Service is rewarded.

Always. Earl Nightingale said, "Your rewards in life are in direct proportion to your service." A lofty idea that sounds so sweet to say. However, service comes disguised as work. Service to others usually requires a little sweat. You should perform your work with a good attitude. But even work performed with a bad attitude gets rewarded. Attitude doesn't get you paid; work gets you paid. Work performed with a good attitude will get you paid better and will make the work go faster and will definitely be more fun, but the key ingredient to doing well is still the work, the effort, and the service.

People who understand that their purpose is service to others and work at providing that service live lives of abundance. Those who don't just live their lives.

If You Want to Have a Better Life . . . Do Something!

"I am doing something! I am busy every day! You have no idea how busy I am!" Okay, I get it. It's not that you are not doing something; you are doing something. You just aren't doing anything productive. You are not serving anyone. You are not helping anyone. You are not really doing anything except sitting on your butt and watching the world go by: the big, cruel world that treats you so badly and keeps you broke and unhappy. Due to your lack of doing the right things, you aren't really successful. You aren't rich. You aren't happy. You're busy. You're working. But you are doing the things that people are willing to reward you for.

What are the right things? I don't believe I need to tell you. You know what they are. You know exactly what you need to do to change your life completely for the better. The problem is never that we don't know; it's always that we don't do what we already know. Remember? I said that earlier when I talked about people being stupid.

So am I totally against motivation and self-help? Not at all. I make my living in that industry. In fact, this is a self-help book.

But look at those two concepts: motivation and self-help. People think of those as separate things. The key is to put those two concepts together. The only way to become motivated is to help yourself. It's up to you: not a book, a CD or DVD, or a speech. And it's not up to any speaker, teacher, television talking head, or preacher either. None of those folks can really motivate you, so don't look to them. Don't count on them. Does that sound strange to hear from a guy who has written five bestsellers, has recorded many audio and video series, is a regular on television talking about this stuff, and has spoken to nearly 400 of the Fortune 500? It may sound strange, but the truth often does. I don't believe any book, speech, or person can really motivate you. Those things can only help you to motivate yourself. However, most motivational tools can't do that for you because their goal is to make you feel good about who you are already. Feeling good about yourself won't move you from where you are to where you want to be.

That is why I say motivation doesn't work. If it did, then motivational speakers would run the world and they would be zillionaires. Trust me, they don't run the world and they are not zillionaires. I don't underestimate the value of what some motivational speakers say; I owe a lot to many of them. But I don't owe any of them for teaching me that feeling good about who I am will make a difference. I do, however, owe a great deal to those who reminded me instead to feel good about what I can do.

FEELING GOOD ABOUT YOURSELF VERSUS BELIEVING IN YOURSELF

This is what you need to understand: Motivation that makes you feel good about yourself won't change your life. Knowing you can achieve what you are willing to work hard enough to make happen will change your life. You have to move from feeling good about yourself to believing in your abilities and taking action on those abilities. There is a major difference between the two concepts. Who cares if you feel good about yourself? Instead, believe in your abilities and take action on them. That concept will propel you to amazing heights.

Most speakers and most books and other programs teach the concept backwards. Many of us have said that in order to have, you must do. And in order to do, you must be. In other words, if I feel good about who I am, then I will be able to do anything.

Heard that before? Well, that might work; in a fairytale world that might work. Our society isn't really the type that will help you feel good about who you are. You are constantly reminded you are just not good enough. You know what? You are never going to feel good enough about yourself to do whatever you want to do. But should that stop you? Hell, no. It isn't about feeling. You are never going to feel you have enough going for you to accomplish anything you want to accomplish. Does it mean that you can't accomplish what you want to accomplish? Absolutely not. You can do just about anything you want to do if you are willing to work hard enough. But you won't do it by feeling good about yourself. In this case, feeling takes a back seat. It takes a back seat to fact. The feeling forced down our throats by the rest of the world and even by ourselves is that we can't. The fact is, you can. So just do it. That's the only way to get it done. You will only do it by doing it. You just have to start. You have to do it and do it and do it. You have to do it badly to begin with. You have to keep doing it until you instill in yourself the courage to do a little more. That is how things get done: by doing something, whether you feel good about yourself or not. And things get done when you take action, whether you have a good attitude about it or a bad attitude. So do something. Anything. Even if you do the wrong thing, you will find out quicker than by not doing anything at all. So do it. Get started. Now.

Self-Image Isn't the Key

Motivational gurus will tell you the key is self-image. The key isn't self-image. Self-image is based on the words "I am." How I feel about myself based on who I am. Well, face it; you are not who you ultimately want to be. Whaaaa! Too bad. Go sit in the corner and whine about it. Maybe you can get on some reality TV show so you can get the whole world to feel sorry for you. That way you can whine about it publicly instead of taking responsibility for it. Surely that will help.

How you feel about who you are just isn't that important. How you feel about what you "can do" is what is important. And you can do just about anything you commit yourself to do based on the best use of your abilities.

I don't give one hoot about who you are or how you feel about yourself. The only thing that's important is what you know you can do once you apply yourself. Once again, let me say you can do just about anything. People have done amazing things. I can show you people with tremendous difficulties to overcome and yet they still accomplish the most incredible things. It doesn't matter who you are or how you feel about who you are, because you rarely feel good enough about yourself to do amazing things. The important thing is to know, without a doubt, that you can do amazing things if you want it badly enough and if you are willing to do whatever it takes to make it happen. You won't do it perfectly—at least not to begin with. But when you begin by doing a little you can build the courage to do more. And with that courage you can do a little more, and then a little more. And then a little more until it's done and something amazing has been accomplished.

That is why motivation alone doesn't work. Motivation typically means that some outside force will inspire you to feel good enough about yourself so you will be able to do anything your little heart desires. Forget it. Instead I say that in order to do anything your heart desires you must know you can do anything you are willing to do. No one is special. It's just that some people have the courage to begin and are willing to risk failure and are willing to continue doing it until it gets done.

You Must Become Uncomfortable

Most people want to make you feel comfortable. I want just the opposite. Big difference, huh? My approach won't make you feel good. And I know how important it is for you to feel good. But feeling good never got you to do anything. If you listen to someone who makes you feel good, I doubt you will ever do a thing. If you listen to someone who makes you feel uncomfortable, then you might do something.

For instance, about 70 percent of our society is overweight. Don't believe me? If not, look down. If that doesn't work, then look around, as it won't take long to find that I am right. There was a time in my life when I was a good 25 pounds overweight. As I gained weight I learned the trick. Just buy bigger clothes and wear a lot of black. That way when you get all dressed up, you can look in the mirror and say to yourself, "You know, I look pretty good!" As long as you convince yourself that you look pretty good, you are never going to lose weight. It's when you are on your way to the bathroom about three in the morning and you catch a glimpse of yourself in the bathroom mirror with your gut and your butt hanging out, and you stop and say to yourself, "Damn, I'm huge!" That is when you are going to do something. Why? Because you are not comfortable with yourself. You don't feel good about yourself. What about when you are walking back from the bathroom and someone you love and trust says to you, "Damn, you are huge!" (And she didn't mean it in a complimentary way!) Then, I guarantee you will do something. Because that is motivation!

Think of me as that trusted loved one who just caught you walking back from the bathroom and I am the one saying to you, "You are huge!" My goal in this book is to make you uncomfortable. Only after you become uncomfortable will you ever begin to change.

Feeling good doesn't create change. Feeling uncomfortable creates change. Why do you change your position in your chair? Because the position you are in is uncomfortable and you are changing it to get more comfortable. If you were not uncomfortable in your current position then you wouldn't move. You would just stay where you are.

I want my words to make you uncomfortable because I want you to change. I want you to discover your best self and go for it. I want you to believe in what you are able to do, to create, to accomplish, and to achieve.

I want to give you a focus and a direction. I want to encourage you to do something. I want you to take action. But it has to be action focused on what you really want. Not the kind of action that has you running around like a chicken with its head cut off.

Focus and Direction

Typically, motivation is a lot like blowing up a balloon. You blow up the balloon and without tying the end, you let it go and it flies all over the room bouncing against everything. While it's great to have a balloon all blown up to play with, to really enjoy it you have to tie off the end so you can really have some fun with it. You can use it like a ball, or rub it on your head and let the static electricity stick it to the wall. Or you can tie a string to it and anchor it to something and bat it around. The possibilities are endless. Without tying off the end you have the frustration of just blowing it up over and over and over again until it finally blows out the window or pops. While that is fun to do for a few minutes, it becomes tiring pretty quickly.

Watch people who have just become all fired up and motivated, but haven't been given any real direction. They are like the balloon that has been blown up but not tied. They bounce around the room letting out lots of motivational hot air, passing out their "Attitude Is Everything" buttons and getting in everyone's way. Yeah, they know all the buzzwords and can quote the jargon, but they have no direction. And just like the balloon, they become tiring after a while.

I watched my son, Tyler, graduate from basic training in the Army. After the ceremony, when they were doing their yells and cheers and all that Army stuff, one of the sergeants yelled out, "Are you motivated?" At this point the soldiers all yelled in unison, "Motivated, motivated, down-right motivated, you check us out, you check us out!" When I asked Tyler about that, he said they all yelled that out at the beginning of any task, assignment, or exercise. Now what is critical to understand is that they already knew the assignment, the task, or the exercise inside and out before they started yelling about how motivated they were. To yell about being motivated with no clue about the task would have been stupid. Why get motivated without a plan? They had a plan, they knew how to do it, and then they got motivated to accomplish it.

Can you see that is the way it should be done? You must have the plan first. To get motivated without a plan is stupid. You are nothing more than a balloon full of hot air. But with a plan the possibilities are endless.

I believe you must have direction: plans, dreams, desires, a picture of what you want, how much you want, who you want, and how you want it to be. You don't need pages of plans; you just need a direction that can be articulated and focused on so you can direct your energy toward it.

OTHER MOTIVATIONAL MYTHS

I have already addressed the myths of having a positive attitude and feeling good about yourself. While those two alone are plenty to keep you from reaching your goals, sadly there are many more we have been fed throughout our lives that are just as detrimental. Here are a few more.

You Can Be Whatever You Want to Be

You've said it before, I know. You've probably told your kids this same thing. It's a lie. Not everyone can be whatever he or she wants to be. Somebody has to do the stuff the rest of us don't really want to do. Not everyone can be a supermodel or a professional basketball player or movie star. First, you may be short, fat, and ugly. That knocks out that supermodel thing pretty quickly. And you may have no talent or skills to become a professional athlete or an actor—although I will admit there are plenty of movie stars with no talent who seem to do pretty well.

You can become whatever you have the potential to become and are willing to dedicate the time and effort into becoming, and what you have the talent for. That is the truth—no more, no less.

You Can Do Whatever You Want to Do

Wrong. Much like the preceding myth, it will only lead to disappointment. You can do whatever you have the talent to do and are willing to work hard enough to make happen. The good news is that you have more talent to do more things than you have given yourself credit for up until now.

You Can Have Whatever You Want to Have

If this were true I would know Halle Berry much better than I do. The truth is you can have whatever you believe you deserve, and whatever you take action toward achieving, utilizing your thoughts, and your words, and your abilities.

The real issue with these three myths is the word want. You don't always get what you say you want; but you do always get what you are willing to work for.

You Become What You Think About

Source: Larry Winget, "Shut Up, Stop Whining, and Get a Life," SmarterComics.

A lie for sure! You don't become what you think about all day long. If that were true, most adolescent boys would be girls. Instead of looking in the mirror and seeing a middle-aged bald guy with earrings and a goatee, I would look in the mirror and see Heidi Klum.

One more time, because it can't be repeated enough: You become what you think about, talk about, and do something about.

Be Yourself

Lousy advice! What if you're stupid? What if you're an asshole? What if you're a stupid asshole? If you're an asshole, stop being yourself and try to figure out how to be someone else—even if it's just a non-asshole version of yourself.

You Are Perfect Just the Way You Are

You don't believe that for a minute. If you believed that, you wouldn't have bought this book. We could debate this issue a good long while, but instead let me give you my take on this myth.

Spiritually it might be true that you are perfect just the way you are. However, on a practical level, you aren't perfect just the way you are. You probably need to change many things about yourself in order for you to be the kind of person the rest of us can put up with.

While God may love you just the way you are, the rest of us won't. We want you to be nice and reasonable and fairly easy to get along with. Otherwise we won't hire you, buy from you, marry you, or be your friend. And you will grow old while being lonely and broke. So wise up and change.

THERE ARE NO PROBLEMS, ONLY OPPORTUNITIES

Source: Larry Winget, "Shut Up, Stop Whining, and Get a Life,"
SmarterComics.

Have you heard that? The motivational types love that one.
What planet are these people from? I have problems. Period.
They are not opportunities. They are problems. And they must be
dealt with like problems. Of course these pie-in-the-sky thinkers
who say this are also the ones who are out there saying, "Every
cloud has a silver lining." Not where I come from. Sometimes the
sky is black and all it does is rain and storm and make a mess. And
sometimes when it storms like that the only thing you can do is
take cover. There is no silver lining ahead; brace yourself for a
tornado!

The folks who say this stuff are well-meaning. I know all they are trying to do is to get you to put it in perspective, and that all bad eventually holds some good. But to cram motivational clichés down your throat when you are facing real issues is insulting.

A problem is a problem. Hurt is real. Pain exists. These are the realities of life. There is no help in sugarcoating them. While every problem can teach us a valuable lesson, it still needs to be called a problem and dealt with like it's a problem.

Give 110 Percent

Just get out there and give it 110 percent! Sure that will do it! No? "Well that is what my boss says to get me to work harder." I know and the self-help bozos love saying this is one of the keys to success. Some of them will even sell you a little lapel pin that has "110%" on it so you can prove to others what a gullible idiot you are.

You can't give 110 percent. It's impossible. One hundred percent is all there is. It's the maximum. There is no 110 percent; it doesn't exist and you cannot give it.

It's like getting on the airplane and having the flight attendant announce the flight is going to be extremely full. No, it isn't. The flight is only full. Full is 100 percent. It can't be more than full. If the flight gets more than 100 percent full, then someone isn't going.

This really isn't a problem for most folks. Very few ever face the challenge of giving more than 100 percent because most people seem to be quite comfortable operating at about 60 percent. Most people work just hard enough so they won't get fired. If you even approach 100 percent, I applaud you. You are in the minority.

However, while you cannot give 110 percent, I will grant you this: You can give more than you think you can. You always have more to give. But you can't give more than there is, and 100 percent is all there is.

Beware of What I Say Here Too

Be careful what you buy into and act upon—even the stuff I am telling you in this book. Try it, and if it works, run with it. If it doesn't, then run from it. If you try what I say here and it doesn't get you the results you are looking for, then dump it and get another book and try something else until you find something that does work for you.

CHAPTER SIX

THE ENJOYMENT FACTOR

"We are put here on earth to fart around. Don't let anyone tell
you any different."

—Kurt Vonnegut

My guess is you aren't having as much fun as you
should have and certainly not as much fun as you could have. If
you are like most people, you don't really think your job is fun,
but you tolerate it or do it because you think you have to or need
to. You probably don't think your friends are all that much fun,
but it just seems like too much effort to find new ones. You might
not even enjoy your spouse all that much. Maybe you don't enjoy
how you dress, the car you drive, or the house you live in. And
there is a very good chance you don't enjoy how you look.

If I am even close to right with any of these statements, then
you need to hear this! I want to change your thinking about
enjoying life. I want you to enjoy every aspect of your life.

STOP DOING THE THINGS YOU DON'T ENJOY DOING

Why do you do things you don't enjoy? Is it because you think
you have to? Well, you don't. Is it because it's expected of you?
I am not buying it. Is it because you have responsibilities? Your
responsibilities are better taken care of when you enjoy yourself.

And your primary responsibility is to be happy! Bottom line: You don't have to do things you don't enjoy. Really.

My Philosophy of Fun and Enjoyment

The overriding principle that rules my life is enjoyment. Some of you may think this statement is self-centered and hedonistic. You could not be more wrong. This statement is actually based on a motive of service to others.

Pay attention to this next part: When you enjoy what you do, you will work hard at becoming excellent at it. When you are excellent at what you do, you will serve others better by doing it well. When you serve others well, you will be rewarded for it.

An absence of enjoyment indicates a presence of frustration and dissatisfaction. Dissatisfaction and frustration lead to negativity, hard feelings, and resentment. Those things will probably cause you to interact negatively with others and in most situations. Which ultimately means you are going to screw up your relationships at home and at work. You will be a jerk to your family. You will be a creep to your co-workers and your customers. You will probably make your boss mad. In the end, you get fired, you lose all your friends, and your spouse or partner will dump you and take all your stuff. You will end up lonely and broke.

Think I am exaggerating? Maybe, though probably not by much. Actually I am just accelerating the process to show you what happens when you don't enjoy your life.

Your Job.   Do you enjoy your job? If not, then quit.

"But, but, but . . ."

No buts about it. Quit. If you don't enjoy what you do, then you probably aren't any good at it. If you aren't any good at it, then you are probably not going to be thought well of at work. And when you go home, you are miserable and do nothing but gripe and complain, which isn't fair to your family.

So either quit your job and find another one or learn to enjoy the job you have. In fact, before you quit, try that. Think about what you do enjoy about your job and focus on that for a while. What you focus on, expands. Which means that if you go to work every day thinking about how much you hate it, you are going to only end up hating it more. And if you go to work looking for something to enjoy about it, even it's just a small thing, you will probably end up enjoying it more. You may just find out that, given a chance, it's a pretty good job after all. I admit that no matter what you do, there will be some aspect of it that isn't as enjoyable as other aspects. However, I won't back down from the idea that overall you must enjoy your job.

One of the smallest groups I ever spoke to had 11 people. There were 10 vice-presidents and the president in the meeting. I made the statement, "When it quits being fun you ought to quit." I took a breath and reached for a drink of water before continuing when one of the vice-presidents interrupted me and said, "Just a minute, Larry—I quit." At that point he stood up and walked out of the meeting. Now that will put a damper on a seminar in a hurry! I suggested we take a short break. After the break, the president of the company came up to me and told me not to say anything like that again. How sad that a man has to become so frustrated with his job he is willing to quit under those circumstances. Can you imagine what he must have been dealing with to quit at that moment and in that way? He later wrote me a letter and told me that after my statement, he felt he had finally been given permission to stop doing what he hated. So he took action.

Not so fast!   It's irresponsible to just quit your job simply because you can't figure out how to like it. Lots of folks go to work every day and do things they don't find fun because they have to pay their bills and provide for their families. There is nothing wrong with that. If that is the case with you, figure out how to make the best of a bad situation until you can ultimately find a job doing something you enjoy. So if you take my advice and quit your job because it isn't fun, that's fine, but make sure you have another job already lined up. I don't want my tax dollars paying your unemployment benefits just because you aren't happy at work.

Your Friends.   Do you enjoy your friends? If not, dump them. Seriously. I am not even going to talk very much about this one. Why spend time with people you don't enjoy? There are plenty of people out there (about 6 billion), so surely you can find a handful of people you enjoy spending time with. I have a personal policy that I won't spend time with people I don't enjoy. That means I don't go to parties or to dinner with people I don't really like. At times that makes me very unpopular with others, including my wife, but very popular with myself. I just won't compromise my personal happiness to put myself in the presence of people I don't like. Selfish? You bet! And I suggest everyone do it.

Your Spouse, Partner, or Significant Other.   Do you enjoy your spouse, partner, or significant other? What are you doing about it? Have you tried? If you have honestly tried and it's just not working, then move on. Again, life is too short to spend it with someone you don't enjoy. If he or she doesn't make your heart soar, move on.

Am I suggesting divorce? Yes. Divorce is better than unhappiness. And don't give me the thing about the kids. No kid ought to have an unhappy relationship as a role model. I take a lot of crap over this one but I will stand by it. I don't think it's right to be in a miserable marriage. It's not right for either of the partners and not right for the kids.

If you aren't legally married and don't enjoy the person you are with, there is no reason to even have a discussion about this. Just move out and move on.

Does this sound harsh to you? It's harsh compared to all those whiney books about the planets (only you enlightened ones will get that) that talk about relationships. Sometimes people stay way too long in a bad relationship. If you find yourself in one, then fix it. Don't bother with who made it bad, and trust me on this one, both of you did. Blaming won't fix it. Get honest with each other. Talk openly about the way you feel and find out how your partner feels. Get help from a third party. Try a little time apart. Distance cools tempers and resentment and provides perspective. Work on it apart and together and with someone else. Then, if it still doesn't do it for you and you can't be happy together, get out.

No one benefits from a bad relationship. No one.

Your Stuff.   Don't enjoy your house? Then move. Can't afford to move? Paint the house. Can't afford to paint it? Move the furniture around. Can't afford furniture? Sleep in the kitchen. Do something to make it different.

Don't like your car? Then why are you still driving it? Sell it or trade it. Can't afford to? Then buy a bicycle or ride the bus!

Don't like what you wear? Buy something different to wear. Can't afford it? Go to the thrift store. The clothes are cheap, and even the stars shop there.

Do you not like your furniture? Garage sale time.

Do you not enjoy the town you live in? Move. I know that sounds drastic. Sometimes it is. It isn't easy to just pick up and move. I used to live in Tulsa, Oklahoma. I was born in Oklahoma and, while I had lived in other places, I ended up there because of family. We all do things like that. We live for others instead of ourselves and we end up unhappy and resentful. Living in Tulsa did not have me at the point of resentment or unhappiness, but I just was not crazy-in-love with living there. Mostly it was the weather. I hate cold weather. My wife, Rose Mary, hates it even more. So I did this little calculation. I was 45 years old. I figured I had about 30 good years left to live if things went pretty well for me. I loved Tulsa four months out of the year. It's a gorgeous place. The weather, the azaleas . . . it's just amazing. The other eight months it's just too cold, or too hot and humid for me. I figured out that I loved where I lived one-third of every year. The other two-thirds weren't working for me. When I applied that two-thirds percentage to the balance of my life I realized I wouldn't like where I was living for 20 years of my next 30. I didn't like those odds. So I moved to Arizona where I love it 10 months out of the year and stay inside the other two months—because it's so hot that dogs explode and burst into flames just walking down the street.

Was it hard? Of course it was hard. I left behind my family and my business and my employees and all I was familiar with. Was it worth it? Absolutely. There is something very gratifying about waking up every day and loving where you live.

Your Appearance. Don't like your appearance? Then change it.

There are things you can do to make you feel better about your appearance:

Get your hair styled differently.

Change the color of your hair.

Get a nose job if you have a big honker.

If your head looks like a '67 Coupe de Ville with the doors open, then get your ears pinned.

Lose some weight, or gain some weight (though I estimate that there are only .001 percent of you that gaining weight applies to).

Get cosmetic surgery if you want to. It's your body and up to you to do what it takes to make you feel good about yourself.

Do whatever it takes to feel good about your appearance. But please guys, don't buy a rug. You will end up looking like you have roadkill on your head regardless of what the salesperson tells you. Trust me, we can tell. Always. And we will laugh; probably not to your face, but we all will behind your back.

Some Irony: Enjoy the Way Things Are

"What?"

Listen to me here. Learn to enjoy things just the way they are. I know it sounds like just the opposite of everything that I have said up until now, but it isn't.

"How can you say that? First you say I must enjoy my life and everything in it and if I don't, then I need to change it. Then when I decide to change my life because I don't enjoy it, you tell me that I am supposed to enjoy it just the way it is! Make up your mind!"

I am not saying things should stay the way they are. I am just saying you should learn to enjoy the way things are while you are in the process of changing them.

Don't become so frustrated by the idea of changing your life so you can enjoy it more, that you forget to enjoy it right now. It's not about the destination; it's about the journey. The way things are right now for you is exactly the way it needs to be for you or at least they're just the way things *are* for you. Enjoy them as best you can.

You might not enjoy things the way they are at the moment, but you are there for a reason. Several years ago I went bankrupt and lost everything. Believe me, there was nothing in that experience that was enjoyable. It was embarrassing. It was demeaning. I lost all my stuff. It sucked! I didn't really mind losing all the money, but I hated losing all my stuff. But it was exactly where I needed to be and what I needed to have happen. I needed the lesson. It was a tough lesson to learn and hard to come to grips with the fact I needed it to happen. But if it hadn't happened, then you wouldn't be reading this book or any of my others. That experience moved me onto a path of growth and learning that resulted in the career I have now helping other people learn from all of my stupid mistakes.

That is what I mean when I say you are where you need to be. I needed that bankruptcy to move me from where I was to where I am. It also taught me to enjoy where I am, regardless of where that is, because whatever is happening to me is happening for a reason. It's there to teach me a lesson. It's a lesson I need to learn to grow to the next level.

You may be having tough times. Lots of people are. I completely understand that those tough times certainly aren't any fun. But there will be a lesson in the experience that you need to learn. Maybe the lesson will be painful and expensive but know it will make you a better person in the long run. Enjoy the idea you are going to be better for having survived the experience.

While that may not seem like much consolation, that may be all you get. Besides, when things are tough just remember one of the most often repeated lines in the Bible: "And it came to pass." That is good news! It did not come to stay; it came to pass.

And don't ever say anything stupid like, "It can't get any worse than this." Trust me. It can always get worse! Regardless of what you are going through, stop and enjoy it. Enjoy it for the simple reason it isn't worse.

CHAPTER SEVEN

YOUR BELIEFS DETERMINE YOUR RESULTS

What you believe about yourself and about the world in general pretty much determines what you have, how much money you make, how healthy you are, and how successful you end up. It determines the quality of your relationships and the quality of your life. I say this because we ultimately act upon what we really believe. If you don't believe you can, you can't. If you believe you can, your chances go way up—it's not guaranteed but you have a definite advantage.

What do you believe? You have a list of things right now you are absolutely sure to be true and that you believe in with all of your heart, mind, and soul. We all do. The list is probably not written down, but it's there. Maybe you never took the time to sit down and really think about your list but that is about to change. I am going to give you a chance to do just that. But first, let me tell you what you believe.

"Wait! You don't even know me. How do you know what I believe?"

It's easy. I can always tell exactly what someone believes. I can tell by looking at your bank account exactly what you believe about money. I can tell what you believe by looking at your car, your house, your shoes, and your clothes. I can tell what you believe about yourself and what you think you deserve. I can tell how hard you work and whether you believe in saving or spending or in a secure financial future. Give me 10 minutes with your bank statement, your credit card statement, and to walk through your house, your garage, and to peek in your closet. That's all it takes for me to know what you believe.

Now you may be saying I'm not being fair. Sure I am. And you may be saying I'm focusing only on the material things to evaluate what I believe. Okay, that's a fair statement. So give me another 10 minutes with your family and another 10 with your friends. By taking a look at your relationships and how you get along with others—your kids, your partner, your friends, and your co-workers—I can sum up what you believe about yourself. I can tell what you believe by how you spend your time alone—what you do when you relax and what you do when you go on vacation. I can tell what you believe by the kind of books you read. I can tell what you believe if you don't read. I can tell what you believe by the television programs you watch and the movies you see. In other words, everything about you—what you do, how you talk, what you have, who your friends are, and where you go—all tell me exactly what you believe. Your beliefs always show up in your life. Without exception, you always are living your belief system.

What you believe about women determines how you treat your wife and how you get along with her. Likewise, what you believe about men determines how you treat your husband and how you get along with him. And what you believe about men and women determines how you treat your son, your daughter, your co-workers, and the strangers you meet. It determines how you vote and how you feel about the people you do business with.

What you believe about yourself determines how you dress—whether your clothes are clean and fashionable and whether you shine your shoes. What you believe about love determines how much of it you give and receive. What you believe about success determines how much of it you have. What you believe about happiness determines if you are happy or not.

Now do you see how I can tell you exactly what you believe by just looking at you and your stuff? Your beliefs leave a trail that shows up in every area of your life.

Look at your life. Take some time to consider the way you live. Think about your belief system and how it affects your possessions, your relationships, your success, and your happiness. Maybe for the first time ever, you'll know why your life is the way it is.

WHAT I BELIEVE

Life is simple. We complicate it and don't need to.

Your results are your own fault.

Love, service, and giving must be the motives of your life.

Money comes to you as the result of serving others.

Service almost always comes disguised as work.

Being healthy is a choice.

People can change but only when they want to and never when you want them to.

Whining and refusing to take responsibility kill your chances of success.

Results never lie.

Most people are lazy and need to get off their butts and do something.

All good is rewarded even though it sometimes takes a long time.

Guilt serves no purpose.

Worry is a waste of time and energy.

Happiness comes only when you rise above the approval of others.

Everything in life gets better when you get better and nothing gets better until you get better.

When it comes to kids, remember: They are your own fault.
Love your work but love it enough to become excellent at it.
It's wonderful to have lots of stuff, but it takes more than
   stuff to make you happy.
Fun should be a way of life, not something you have from
   time to time.
Everything in life is a lesson. Refusing to learn the lesson
   means that it will be repeated until the lesson is learned.
Better to do without today so you can have plenty tomorrow.
Life is short—don't waste it in front of the television.
In the long run, none of this really matters much anyway so
   there is no need to get your panties in a wad.

I am big on lists. In a moment I want you to make a list of
what you believe, but first you can look at my list above to see
what I believe.

That isn't all I believe. But it's the core of what I believe and
live my life by. Now make your own list about what you believe
on the lines that follow.

After making your list, do you see how what you believe has
affected your results? Look at your life and try to determine what
belief you have that has created and supported that result. If you
are not happy with your results, change your beliefs.

WHAT I BELIEVE

_____

_____

_____

_____

_____

Know Thyself!

That's an ancient Greek aphorism that basically means, "Figure out who you are." Years ago, I figured that the only way to be happy was to figure out who I am, accept it, stand by it, and let it be. If people like who I am, fine, we can be friends or we can do business. If people don't like who I am, then that's fine too, we don't have to be friends and we don't have to do business. It really is that simple. Problems arise when people spend too much time and put too much effort into being the person others want them to be. This goes way beyond the criticism factor I have been talking about. This isn't about seeking the approval of others but about living your life trying to be someone you aren't. This is a sure-fire way to be miserable.

I don't have a formula to teach you how to be yourself. In my case, when I realized I was miserable from trying to be the person others wanted me to be, I just gave it up. I gave up saying what others wanted me to say, dressing the way others thought I should dress, and being the person they wanted me to be. I just quit. No magic formula or strategy. I just knew I hated the person I had become: their version of Larry. People often asked me how I did it. I don't know. For a while the transformation was gradual and then it was pretty dramatic. It's kind of like that old story about Michelangelo when he carved the statue of David. When asked how he knew David was in that block of stone, Michelangelo replied that he removed everything from the stone that wasn't David and what was left was David. Or something like that. I don't know if the story is true but it's still a good story and a prime example of what I am talking about here. I just went about dumping the things that weren't me until eventually, what was left was me.

You should try it yourself. Start dumping the things that feel in conflict with who you really are. The beliefs that don't serve you well, the ideas that are keeping you stuck, the people that you have nothing in common with and don't like that much anyway. Become authentic. It's the most freeing thing you will ever do for yourself. Here's an idea: Write down who you are. Don't think about anyone else reading it, as that will just bring judgment and approval of others into the equation. Just write it and then begin to become it.

WHO AM I?

_____

_____

_____

_____

_____

_____

_____

_____

_____

_____

CHAPTER EIGHT

FITNESS, FATNESS, AND MORE

Americans have become the fattest society on earth. By 2020, 75 percent of Americans will be clinically obese. By 2050, one-third of us will have diabetes and the top contributor is obesity. For the first time in history we are raising a generation of children who are not going to outlive their parents. Medical costs for obesity are already through the roof and will only go up and get worse. And medical expenses are the number one cause of bankruptcy. Over 300,000 adult deaths per year in the United States alone are directly attributable to unhealthy eating habits and a sedentary lifestyle. All because people can't stop eating like pigs and won't move. Hundreds of thousands of mothers, fathers, sons and daughters, sisters and brothers will deprive their family of their existence because they won't stop eating and won't move. I want to make it clear I am not an expert in this area, but I know this: Nothing will contribute more to your health than a proper diet and exercise. We are going to spend $40 billion in the diet industry this year when much of it could be solved with a walk and by putting down the fork. But you know most of that already, right? Few people really don't understand or won't agree that proper diet and exercise will help them lead a longer, healthier life.

"Larry, this is ridiculous! What is the problem with people?" What it is the problem? Stupidity, I guess.

PEOPLE ARE STUPID

"So you think people are stupid?" No. I don't think people are stupid. I know people are stupid. I wrote a *New York Times* best-seller called *People Are Idiots and I Can Prove It* that broke down just how stupid people are. Interesting though, idiots found that title offensive, so when it came out in paperback, it was changed to *The Idiot Factor*. Guess you can't really call people idiots or stupid and have them love you. Oh well, better to tell the truth and let them work it out for themselves.

However, I would like to explain what I mean by the word "stupid." If you don't know any better, then you are ignorant. If you know better and still do it, then you are stupid. Big difference. I will forgive you (for a while) for not knowing any better. But once you know what you are doing and you do nothing about it, then you are stupid—and there is no forgiveness for knowing better and still doing it in spite of having the knowledge.

If you don't believe me when I say people are stupid, I would love to prove it to you.

Stupidity Factoid #1

We eat things we know aren't good for us. Things that make us fat, clog our arteries, raise our cholesterol, and do lots of other harmful things. Even after we are diagnosed with these problems and told exactly what we should and shouldn't eat, we still eat the stuff that is bad for us. Stuff that will eventually kill us. Do you call that intelligent behavior? I call it stupid.

Here is something interesting: According to most religious beliefs, suicide is a sin. Why is it that taking a gun, shooting yourself in the head, and ending your life in a split second is a sin, but overeating or smoking and killing yourself over a 30-year period isn't? The end result is the same. So it must not be killing yourself that is really a sin after all. It must be how long it takes to do it. I know, let's ask one of those fat television evangelists that question.

Stupidity Factoid #2

People put things that are full of carcinogens and other toxins in their mouths and light them up and suck hot fire and smoke down into their lungs. Studies say that every cigarette you smoke ends your life 13 minutes sooner. Yet, knowing this, cigarette use continues to rise. Does that sound like an intelligent interpretation of the facts to you? Sounds pretty stupid to me. Even after being diagnosed with cancer, or emphysema, or some other terminal problem, and people are told that the only way to live is to quit smoking, many still continue to smoke. Could you call that anything but stupid?

Of course the simple thing to do is to sue the company that makes the cigarette because they made a product that gave you cancer. How smart is that? They did not give you anything; you gave it to yourself. You willingly went out and spent your own money, stuck the cigarette in your mouth, and fired it up. You did it not once, but thousands upon thousands of times. You must have wanted cancer. The tobacco company printed the warning on the label telling you that you could get cancer if you smoked their cigarettes and you still bought them and smoked them anyway. You knew they would kill you and you still did it, and then you whine about what someone else did to you. Take responsibility for your choices—you made them. Live with them or die with them but either way, know those were your choices.

Stupidity Factoid #3

Drink too much alcohol and you can't drive. Your judgment is impaired and your reaction time is slowed down. All of this is proven; it's not up for argument because it's fact. Yet, people still get drunk and get behind the wheel of their car and drive. Sometimes they kill themselves. Sadly, they usually just kill others. Yet they knew they were impaired when they started out. But they did it anyway. Again, would you call this intelligent behavior?

Get the point yet? People are stupid. Humans are the only creatures on the planet that spend every day doing things they know will only bring about their own destruction. People know they are killing themselves by how they eat, drink, smoke, and behave, yet they do it anyway. What would you call that? I call it stupid.

In addition, people know they are killing their own planet—the place they live—yet they do it anyway. See any other living thing doing that? No other creature willingly, knowingly, laughingly destroys its environment.

We continually do things we know are exactly the wrong things to do; things that are not good for us emotionally, financially, physically, and psychologically. That is stupid.

"Only two things are infinite, the universe and human stupidity, and I'm not sure about the former."

—Albert Einstein

"Okay Larry, aren't you ever stupid?"

Absolutely. There are times that I consider myself the poster child for stupidity. I have made every mistake in the book. I just try not to make them over and over again when I know better. Knowingly doing the wrong thing over and over again at the expense of your success, prosperity, family, or health is stupid. So stop being stupid—in all areas, but especially when it comes to being healthy.

BELIEVE IN HEALTH

Stop buying into the idea you have to be unhealthy. You don't. Everyone, regardless of their current condition, can improve their condition by changing their state of mind regarding their condition. Again, this isn't new-agey mumbo jumbo—science will back up that when you think differently about your condition, you can alter your condition. I'm not spewing spontaneous healing here, so don't go crazy on me.

Stop believing the commercials on television about the arrival of cold and flu season. It's not true. While there is a time of year when people are more susceptible to catching a cold than at other times, you don't have to be one of the people who catches a cold. It never has to be cold and flu season for you. The idea that you are going to catch a cold just because the weather has turned a little chilly is a myth sold to you by the people who make drugs they want you to buy. It's marketing. If you stopped buying into the idea of the cold and flu season and quit thinking it's inevitable you are going to catch a cold, then you would stop experiencing the cold and flu season and you would stop having colds.

So am I saying you can just think your way to health? Yes, in many cases that is exactly what you can do. However, a healthy diet and exercise are a part of it too. You can't think healthy while you overeat and smoke and expect to be healthy. Use your head on this one!

Mom and Migraines

If you have ever experienced a migraine you know how debilitating it can be. My mother had been afflicted with migraine headaches—the kind that put you down for days. She had suffered from them for 50 years. But then, my father was diagnosed with colon cancer. He got very ill and needed her care. She decided she could no longer have migraine headaches because she had to take care of my dad and there simply wasn't time for one. They were simply a luxury that she could not afford any longer. So she gave them up. Simple as that. She chose to stop having them and never had one again. Years after he died she told me this story about giving up migraines. I was incredulous. I had also suffered for most of my life with migraines, as had my sister. It appears they are hereditary so we all dealt with them. When my mother told me this story, I decided right then and there that I never had to have a migraine headache again either. I told myself "If she can do it, then I can do it!" So I did it. I made up my mind that I didn't ever need a migraine again. And I have never had another one. Simple as that. I made a choice and created an expectation, and as a result never had another migraine.

That kind of thinking will work for you, too. *If* you believe it. Over the years I have gotten some flack over this story. People say it won't work. They are absolutely right. It won't work. For them. But it worked for me because I believed it would.

Exercise

This is a tough one for most people. They would rather die than exercise. So they do. Exercise programs are not what most people think they are. You don't have to go to the gym and pump yourself up like a bodybuilder.

Healthy exercise mainly consists of aerobic exercise—anything that increases your heart rate for a period of 20 minutes at least three times a week. That isn't that tough. A bicycle ride, a walk, a jog, a run, or wild crazy sex for 20 minutes (yeah right—20 minutes!).

I am not an expert in this area, so go to a gym and hire a personal trainer or at the bare minimum get some good books or do some research on the Internet—and talk to your skinny doctor first.

Doctors and Health

Find a skinny doctor who doesn't smoke. Do I even need to explain this one? Just in case I do, how could you even consider going to a doctor who is overweight, smokes, and doesn't take care of himself? That makes no sense!

Find a doctor who will suggest proper eating and exercise and natural remedies before he suggests drugs. Drugs did not make you sick (unless you are a drug addict), and chances are that drugs aren't the best first resort either. I will bet it was your diet and lack of exercise that made you sick in the first place, so start there. Want to know if that might be the case? Strip down naked and look in the mirror; that will give you some of your answer. (Again, not all the time folks. But certainly a good part of the time!)

Does doing all that homeopathic, natural stuff sound strange and weird to you? I find it interesting that cutting a person open sounds more logical and makes more sense to some people than diet, exercise, and natural remedies. That says a lot about conditioning ourselves for stupidity.

Stop Being Fat

I have a prejudice against fat. I will readily admit it. I have no prejudices against race or sexual orientation—you have no choice regarding those things. I do, however, have a prejudice against stupidity, laziness, and being fat—with fat being the result of both stupidity and laziness. Those three things are choices.

I come from a big family. I don't mean big because there are lots of people, I mean I come from a big family because they are *big* people. Are they predisposed to being big? No. They have poor eating habits and don't exercise. Period. They are not alone. As I have already established, many people eat poorly and are dangerously overweight. I could be. It wouldn't take a month for me to become a total lard butt. I love the taste of everything that is bad for me to eat. Fatty foods simply taste good. The bad stuff seems to have the most flavor. And I love it all. I think gravy and chocolate should be two of the main food groups. But I won't become fat. I won't become fat out of self-respect.

I believe that one of the reasons fat people become fat and stay fat is lack of self-respect. Plus, in my case, I have mouthed off too much to ever become fat. I would lose all credibility if I didn't live the way I preach others should live. And putting all that talk out there into the world sets a bar in place that I must live up to. You should try that. Just get real mouthy about something and then the sheer embarrassment of not performing to your own standard will keep you from falling below the bar you have set. My prejudice against fat people stems from my knowledge that I could easily be the same way and have even been close to being the same way a few times, and now have to literally work my butt off not to be that way. When you work hard at something, exercising discipline and denial, then combine that with a little sweat, you become very intolerant of those who don't. And please don't think I am fit because I love exercise and love eating right—I hate it. But I hate being fat even more.

There seems to be a controversy going on now about obesity. Is it a condition or a disease? I have watched a lot of news coverage dealing with that question. My answer is that it's neither a condition nor a disease. It's a choice. It's your choice to eat the way you do. After all, did you ever eat anything by accident?

Lose Weight the Larry Way

There are countless diets out there. There is the Monkey Chow Diet, the Baby Food Diet, the Shoe Diet, and many other stupid diets. There are about as many stupid diets as there are stupid people. People are desperate to lose weight it seems. (At least to the tune of about $40 billion a year.) Diets don't work. You can't go on a diet and lose weight. At least not long term.

Many studies have already proven this to be true. Again, folks, please don't bother to argue when you don't have a clue what you are talking about! Weighing the right amount is about a lifestyle, not yo-yoing up and down with diets.

There are only two healthy ways to lose weight: Eat smarter and exercise more. Period. While of course you should visit your skinny doctor before beginning any diet or exercise program, let me give you my nonmedical advice for losing weight and becoming healthier.

- Stop going to fast food restaurants as often. They make their living selling grease. They have to use grease to cover up the fact that they are not serving you much real food. Don't kid yourself; grease tastes good. I like it. And it's okay every once in a while but you can't do it every day. And don't use convenience or price as an excuse, because fast food restaurants are rarely fast and they certainly aren't cheap. And don't let the Dollar Menu fool you either—yeah, it's a dollar but you will pay the price with your waistline.
- Leave the parking spaces close to the door for really old people and wimps. You need to walk. Park as far away as you can without having to cross a major thoroughfare on foot. (Fat people don't run across streets well.)
- Take your dog, your kid, or your partner for a walk—even if it's just around the block. It's good for your body and promotes conversation, making it also good for your relationship—even with the dog.
- Don't weigh too often. If you weigh yourself every day you'll get discouraged. You didn't gain all of your weight in a day and you can't expect to lose it all in a day. Don't set unrealistic expectations and then become discouraged because you don't drop pounds on a daily basis. Weekly weigh-ins are plenty often enough to check progress.

- Smaller portions are key. People just eat too much food. Regardless of where you eat or what you eat, eat less of it. Just this morning, I went to a restaurant for breakfast and I ordered a short stack (two pancakes). Seemed like a reasonable breakfast. The short stack was short, only about an inch high but the pancakes were bigger than the 10-inch plate they were served on. They had enough butter on top to lather up a fat boy at the beach. Sadly, most people would ooh and ah and talk about what a great place this breakfast restaurant was for that reason alone. In fact, it's lauded to be one of San Diego's best places to eat breakfast. Yet I always wonder whether restaurants are being praised for the quality of their food or for the quantity? Seems like in America, for a restaurant to be considered good, it has to serve ginormous portions—to hell with quality.

    My wife and I ate at a popular Italian restaurant recently that everyone said was just the best place ever. When they delivered our food, there must have been 10,000 calories in front of us. Seriously, there was enough food for six grown people. My piece of lasagna was at least 8 × 8 and 4 inches thick; enough to serve four people alone. It was disgusting. It tasted okay but holy crap, what one person needs that much food? Yet, if they brought only enough food to fill a person up or to be healthy, they would go out of business for being stingy and serving skimpy portions. Instead they load you up with mediocrity and astound you with their huge portions. I have been lucky enough to travel all over the world—nowhere does this happen like it does in America. In Europe, the focus is on how good the food is, how tasty it is, not about how much of it you can stack on a plate. They don't concern themselves with calories . . . yet Europeans aren't fat like Americans. Why? Portion control.

- When you lose a significant amount of weight, buy something new to wear that is expensive. You will feel like a million bucks and you will be very reluctant to gain the weight back to the point where you can't wear your new purchase.
- When you lose a little weight, go to the tailor and have your good clothes taken in. (I said good clothes; dump the ones that aren't so good.) You'll be proud of yourself for having things taken in instead of let out like you have been doing. And when you lose a little weight don't forget to rub your fat friends' noses in it. However, this can be particularly bad if you gain the weight back. So don't gain it back and don't be a complete jerk about the weight you are losing. It's better to eat good food than bad words.
- Don't think fat, and don't think fit. In fact, don't think. If you focus on your weight, it will become an obsession and make you hungry or make you have angst about what you could have done or should be doing or have eaten or didn't eat or ate too much of. Simply do what you know is right, eating healthy foods and exercising. The weight will take care of itself.
- Don't beat yourself up for slipping. And you *will* slip. If you are absolutely going crazy for a pizza, then eat it. Enjoy it completely. Then adjust tomorrow and the next day. Just don't allow yourself to go crazy very often. Little indulgences should never become regular occurrences.
- When you splurge, do it in front of a toilet or wastebasket. (I said splurge, not purge! I'm not endorsing bulimia.) This trick has helped me a lot. When I want something like a bag of M&M's, then I buy a bag of M&M's. I open it in front of the toilet or a trashcan and after eating a few—just enough to get the taste and the crunch, which is all I really wanted in the first place—I flush them or throw the rest

away in the trash. Suggestion: Use a public trash can so you won't dive in for them later. I've actually done that! See why the toilet works better?

- Find a skinny buddy to eat with. Not a fat buddy. Not a person who will tempt you with fattening food or take you to places you know you shouldn't be. Eat with someone who shares your common goal and will encourage you to eat right.

- When you're hungry, stay away from places like the food court at the mall and the grocery store. If you need to go out and you know it's to a place where you will be tempted, then drink a huge glass of water before you go to help fill yourself up. Grocery shopping when you are hungry is also just dumb.

- Willpower is totally overrated. I admit that I don't have much. I have a problem saying no to things I enjoy. Denial is just not my style. Indulgence is more my style. I bet you are the same way. Here is what works for me: lack of opportunity. Don't have things that aren't good for you available for easy access. Limit your food options. Don't fill your cabinet with cookies and then try to deny yourself. When eating in a restaurant, ask the waiter not to leave the breadbasket and not to bring the dessert menu. Don't tempt yourself unnecessarily.

- When you stop for gasoline, pay at the pump. That way you won't be tempted to buy a soda or candy bar when you go inside to pay.

- Drink lots of water. Carry a bottle of water with you all of the time. It will fill you up and keep your system flushed. This is especially important when eating out. Always ask for a glass of water and drink it before you order. Fill up a little so you won't be quite as hungry when you order and won't have as much room in your stomach when the food comes. Then keep drinking the water throughout the meal.

- Stop lying to yourself and everyone else. You don't have a glandular problem. The percentage of people in the world who actually have one is so small they don't even count. And you are not "big boned." Your frame may be larger than others but your bones are not the problem; the fat you pack on those bones is the problem. And don't say, "My family is heavy; we are just heavy people." That is no excuse. Chances are your problem isn't hereditary. The reason your family is fat is that they eat like pigs and sit on their fat butts. Period. You grew up thinking that was normal. You probably think everyone puts gravy on cereal. It isn't in your genes. You probably haven't been able to fit in your jeans for a good long while.
- Turn off the TV, get off your fat butt, and do something. You need to walk or ride a bicycle, or have sex—anything that makes your heart beat a little faster. It doesn't take a gym or any fancy equipment. It takes movement.
- Go to a gym. I know I just said that you don't have to go to a gym, and you don't. But if you are serious about being healthy, then a gym is a must. You need to lift some weights. You don't have to look like a bodybuilder but you do need to build muscle. Muscle burns calories faster than fat, even at rest. It speeds up your metabolism. Plus gyms are full of people who share a similar goal: They want to be healthier.

NOW LET'S GET REALLY UGLY ABOUT YOUR HEALTH

You say you love your family. Okay, I believe you. Well, sort of. Almost. Okay, not really.

Let me explain my doubt. Do you love them enough to get healthy? Enough to do what it takes to live as long as you can so you can take care of them, enjoy them, and be with them?

Perhaps you love them but just not quite enough to give up cigarettes. Even though you know that every cigarette you smoke shortens your life up to 13 minutes. What could you do in 13 minutes? Could you play catch with your son? Hug your little girl? Make love to your spouse or partner? Could you laugh together, play together, or just enjoy being together? Think about the last time you really had fun with your family. Remember the very best part of the day and realize that time might have lasted only 13 minutes. Would you give up those 13 minutes in order to smoke a cigarette? You would trade that wonderful time just to light one up? I hope not. Yet every day you smoke shortens your life and denies you and your family the fun and love you share together.

Now on to fat people . . . is that candy bar more important to you than your kids? Did you really need to super-size the fries? Are you willing to die for those fries? Fat people die quicker than fit people. And even if they don't die, their quality of life suffers because they are overweight. Is a diminished life evidence of your love?

Heart disease and cancer are the number one and number two killers in our society. Yet they are both diseases primarily chosen to be experienced because people aren't willing to stop smoking, stop eating like pigs, or stop sitting on their big fat butts.

How can you look your family in the eye and tell them that a cigarette or the fettuccine alfredo is more important to you than they are? Can you really do that? You do it every time you light up and every time you pack on the fat. You don't use words to say it; you use a fork or a pack of smokes, but the message is still very clear. You love your self-destructive lifestyle more than you love your family. You are selfish.

CHAPTER NINE

EVERYONE SCREWS UP

"Larry, my life is a mess! I have screwed everything up!"

I get hundreds of e-mails every month just like this. People who have money problems, job problems, relationship problems, and health problems. When I get them, I'm glad to at least see that these folks admit they have a problem. You can't take responsibility for a problem until you admit you have one.

Let's get this straight: Of course you have problems. Everyone does. I have problems too. If you reach the point you don't have any problems, know that you are dead! So stop thinking you are special because you have a problem. Shut up about it. No one wants to hear it (unless you pay them to listen). Besides, they have problems of their own to deal with.

Besides, your problems are your fault. Yes, your fault. For the most part, your actions created the mess you are in. And even if something horrible happened that you honestly had nothing to do with, your reaction to that problem is still your fault. The key is to deal with your problem as a problem so you can move from problem to solution until the next problem comes along.

BEAT YOURSELF UP... BUT NOT FOR LONG

Believe me, I want you to beat yourself up for being stupid. I want you to feel bad. I want you to cry and add some emotion to your stupidity. I want genuine remorse. But not for long. Taking responsibility isn't about wallowing in your stupidity. It's about recognizing that you have made mistakes, admitting to yourself and the other people involved that you are responsible and that you are sorry and then about putting the remorse behind you and taking action to find a solution.

A Smart Kid

One day as I was walking out of the back door of my house to leave on a speaking engagement, my older son, Tyler, said to me, "Dad, I have yet to figure out why anybody would pay you to come and talk to them." I thought, "What a nice thing for you to say!" Then he proceeded to tell me how he had been listening to me speak for years and just didn't get it. He reminded me that I prided myself on telling people how simple life is. He said, "Dad, I live with you and you've complicated your life just like everyone else." He told me that he had figured out exactly what it took to be successful. I said to him, "Of course, you have, you are 19 years old, just got fired from your job, just flunked out of your first semester of college, and just totaled your car, obviously you have all the answers." I asked him to share with me what, in his opinion, it took to be successful. He answered me with, "When you mess up . . . big deal. Just admit it, fix it, and move on. Other than that, life's a party!"

"When you mess up . . . big deal. Just admit it, fix it, and move on. Other than that, life's a party!"

—Tyler Winget

You know what? My son is right. It's really that simple. I have given you an entire book about how to live your life and he boiled it all down into just one little sentence. I hate that!

Big Deal. In my seminars I ask, "How many of you have ever messed up before?" Everyone raises their hands. Because everyone messes up. I shout out, "Big deal!" Then I ask, "How many of you plan on messing up again?" Some will raise their hands but many will shout back, "I don't *plan* on it!" If you don't plan on messing up, then you don't plan on doing much in your life. If you are ever going to do anything, you are going to mess it up. It happens, big deal. You aren't immune from messing up unless you never do a damn thing.

Admit It. Gee, I think that's called taking responsibility. That's the one thing few people are willing to do. We would rather blame others for our problems than ever admit that we caused them. Yet no progress in life really comes until you admit your mistakes and own them. If my son got that from me and that's the only thing he ever learned, then I was a pretty good daddy.

Fix It. This can be a tough one for some people as they were never taught the process for problem solving. To fix a problem you must admit you have one. Then you should write the problem down so you will know what you are really dealing with, not what you just think you are dealing with. This will keep you from disasterizing the problem and making it worse than it really is. Then break the problem down into small manageable pieces. Some problems are too big to handle all at once and need to be attacked in portions. Then focus on the solution. Yes, don't focus on your problem, just the solution.

Move On. People love to wallow in their problems. That is why we have support groups full of people who want to wallow with us. We like to recant the problem, cry about it, hash it, rehash it, talk about it, think about it, analyze it, become introspective about it, meditate on it, write about it, journal it, blog about it, put it on Facebook and tweet it, even possibly sue someone else because we have it... everything, no *anything*, but fix it and move on!

"Are you trashing my support group?"

Have I been unclear here? Yes! I am. I am trashing your support group. I have yet to see one that really helps people by saying, "You messed up . . . big deal! Admit it, take responsibility for it, fix it, get over it, and move on to the next thing!" If you are a part of a support group that practices a philosophy like the one I just described, then please accept my most humble apology. However, if you're part of a support group where everyone gets together and wallows in the misery of each other's problems, then get the hell out of that group now! Dump the whiney losers and find some real friends. And if you have one of those idiot life coaches who allows you to whine and cry and feels sorry for you, dump him too. Life coaches can be certified on the Internet for only $99 and most of the ones I have encountered lead pretty sad lives. Ever heard the saying, "The blind leading the blind?" Welcome to the wonderful world of life coaching! (Go ahead and write me, life coaches. I've said it before and will continue to say it: If you don't have a great life then you can't coach another person to have one.)

> You can circle up, hug, hold hands, and sing Kum Ba Yah for the rest of your life, but until you shake it off and get started on the process of creating a new life you are going to remain miserable.

A good life coach or support group won't tolerate your whining. Neither will a real friend. A real friend would never say to you, "That's okay, sweetie, it's a tough world out there and you have been beat up by it. You poor thing, come here and cry on my shoulder." A real friend will grab you by the shoulders and shake you and remind you that you are able to deal with anything. He will tell you that he will help you get over and get past what you are dealing with. He won't tolerate your BS and will remind you that you are in control of your own life. He will tell you that you created your own mess and only you can create something better if you will just shut up, get over it, and get started!

That's a friend. A friend will help you fix it and move on!

CHAPTER TEN

GET SMARTER

On average, people spend about 100 hours per year reading. Yet they spend nearly 2,000 hours per year watching television. Forty hours a week in front of the tube and only two hours a week looking at something with words on it—how can this be?

According to the American Booksellers Association:

- Eighty percent of Americans did not buy or read a book this year. (Congratulations: By buying and reading this book you are already in the top 20 percent of all Americans.)
- Seventy percent of American adults haven't been in a bookstore in the last five years.
- Fifty-eight percent of American adults never read a book after high school.
- Forty-two percent of university graduates never read another book.

Another study reports only 14 percent of our society will go in a bookstore or a library and actually walk out with a book, and only 10 percent of those people will read past the first chapter.

Is it any surprise that we are in the mess we are in? People are getting dumber every year. Our school test scores are evidence of that. Fewer people are reading and more people are stupid. Is there a correlation?

Want to have some fun? Ask people you know to name the last five books they've read. If they can name one it will be amazing. I promise, it's great fun! Then ask them what book they are currently reading. I'll bet you nine out of ten are not reading anything. By the way, here is a success tip for you: Don't associate with people who don't read. Seem cruel to dump people simply because they don't read? It's more cruel to yourself to hang around people who are dumb.

HOW TO READ A BOOK

"I know how to read a book, Larry. You don't have to tell me." Everyone knows how to read a book. You pick it up and start reading. I get that. But I want you to get the most out of your books so they will have a lasting impact on your life. Some folks love electronic books. That's great. Personally, I'm old fashioned and like to hold a book with pages. It might be my age, it might be that I'm technologically challenged, and it might be that because I write books, I think of them differently than most folks. Whether you buy an electronic book or a regular book with pages, follow these principles as best you can to get the most out of your books.

1. If at all possible, buy the book. Libraries are great resources for reference material and for fiction you don't care about keeping after you have read the book. But when you are investing in a book that has life-changing information in it (things you will want to refer to over and over again), you need to buy the book. If you simply can't afford to buy the book, then go to the library and check it out. However, on the way to the library, kick yourself in the butt for being so broke you can't afford a book! (There are lots of great used bookstores that sell wonderful books at bargain prices. I recently saw one of mine in a used bookstore for a quarter. What a deal!)

2. If the book is yours, mark it up. Write your name in it. Get a highlighter and mark the parts that really speak to you. Make margin notes. When you've finished the book, go to the back of the book, find one of the blank pages, and summarize what you learned from that book. In fact, begin this new habit by doing it in this book!

3. Tell everyone what a great book you're reading. This will reinforce what you are learning. It's also a great way to boost your own ego because it's doubtful they have read any books recently, so you can be proud and brag that you have. Plus it might encourage them to buy a book and read it.

4. Don't loan anyone your books. If you loan someone your book you deprive her of the privilege of marking the parts that mean something to her, therefore diminishing the impact the book will have on her life. Plus, you probably won't get the book back. If it's a book that really has spoken to you, you will want it back. Instead, buy her a copy of the book for her very own. This is a sign of generosity and exhibits your giving nature and inflicts on her a sense of obligation that might encourage her to actually read the book.

5. Buy lots of books. Go to the bookstores to browse and when a book title speaks to you, buy it—even if you don't have time to read it right now. Have a "to be read" shelf: a stack of books just waiting to be read. Always have a few books waiting on you.

6. Read several books at the same time. I have books I take on the airplane when I know I have a few hours of uninterrupted time. I also have books by my bed I use to relax me and help me to fall asleep. I have books full of quotes and very short chapters, which I read when I only have a few minutes. I have books that cover heavy subjects that I read when my mind is fully alert and can focus well, and books that are light and don't require a great deal of concentration. Have a variety of books available that fit the time, the place, and your mood.

7. Don't hesitate to stop when you find yourself with a bad book in your hand. You may get 25 pages into a book and decide it has nothing to say to you. Put it down and get another. Don't do that with this book, though; wait for the next one to begin that practice.

8. Read for different reasons. Read to learn. Read to lift your spirits. Read for pure entertainment. Any book is better than most television.

What Should I Read?

Here is a clue: Don't read what poor people read. Know why? You don't want to be like them. Read what rich people read. Why? You want to be like them. Is this stuff simple or what?

However, be careful. The self-help section of the library and the bookstores is full of quacks who have written books just to sell books instead of trying to help people. Some of the bestselling books today are total garbage. A bestseller isn't necessarily an indication of a great book.

For instance, there was a bestselling book on the market that has a chapter that says "nice managers get better results." Absolute hogwash. Being nice has nothing to do with results; no more than being mean has anything to do with results. Results are never about nice or mean. Results come from clearly communicating what is expected from the employees, training them to do the job, and then staying involved enough to make sure the job is actually being done. When it is, you reward the employee; when it isn't, you discipline the employee. In a nutshell, that is the job of a manager. Whether you are a nice manager or a mean manager isn't important. It comes down to doing your job. Managers who do their job get results.

There is another book out there that topped the bestseller lists from a chef who says that the key to leadership is to forget making sure the customer is happy and instead focus on making your employees happy. Is this guy crazy? Who cares if your employees are happy? It's impossible to make an employee happy anyway! (More on that later.) Focus on making the customer happy because it's the customer's money that keeps you in business. How long is good ol' chef going to be able to keep his restaurant open with happy employees and unhappy customers? Remember this: The customer is *revenue* and the employee is an *expense*.

See how stupid some of this stuff can be? People are selling stuff that makes absolutely no sense! Yet people buy it. Because it looks and sounds new, it sounds like a secret that no one else has said yet and it must be right for that reason alone.

Let me make this clear: There are no secrets. None. There is no new information. What it took to be successful a thousand years ago is exactly what it takes to be successful today. I only remind people of the stuff that eons of data have proved to be true. That is information you can trust. Information that is tried, tested, and true. But that information doesn't always sell because it doesn't have the same sizzle as the new stuff. And success must be a secret since it has managed to elude people for so long. So sell it as new and say it's a secret and you are almost guaranteed bestseller status. Bottom line: Be careful when you shop for books. Find a book that speaks to you, then follow that writer and try his other books. Hey, that's a great idea! If you like one of my books, check out my others.

It Takes More Than Books

While books are about the easiest source of learning in my opinion, don't limit your learning to only books. There are many other ways to get smarter.

Audio Learning. I have listened to more than 5,000 hours of audiotapes (back when we had audio tapes) and compact discs by some of the world's leading speakers and authors. If you travel a lot and have plenty of road time you can take advantage of this great way to learn. Practically every book is also available on audio, either on CD or as a download for your MP3 player. Almost all of the great speakers, lecturers, and trainers offer their material on compact disc or downloadable. I sure do. You can get dozens of hours of Larry Winget and I can yell this stuff at you all the time!

Video Learning. Another great way to learn from great speakers is to see them on video. This is one of my favorite ways to learn, as I like to watch people while they talk to me. Most speakers, trainers, and lecturers have lots of video available. (Again, I do, so go online and get some of it!) Plus, the Internet has tons of free video available on youtube.com and other sources.

Seminars. Your city is probably full of opportunities for you to go hear speakers, trainers, and lecturers deliver high-quality, content-rich seminars on nearly any subject you can think of. The key is you have to go. Pay the money for a ticket and take advantage of these opportunities.

Talk to Smart People. Finally, my favorite method for getting smarter: Ask people who know what you want to know to share what they know. They will more than likely be willing to do it. Ask a rich guy what he did to get rich. Chances are in your favor he will give you a couple of minutes. Don't be a nuisance and don't take too much time. Just ask, say thank you, and move on. He will appreciate your interest and you will have a nugget you can act on. But here is a word of caution: Don't argue with him. When he tells you what he did to get rich or become successful, don't argue and say things like "that won't work for me." I'm always amazed when people who aren't successful feel they have the right to argue with those who are successful. These people obviously don't know what they are talking about or they would be successful themselves. Instead, they should just shut up and listen and learn something. Don't ask a person who is successful or rich to defend his position. He doesn't have to; it obviously works, as he is rich and successful. Sadly, this is why most successful people end up cutting themselves off from those who aren't. They are tired of defending themselves. So if you get one of those rare moments where you get the chance to ask someone her key to success, be respectful, be interested, and be appreciative. That way, she may let you ask again another time.

If you are hesitant to ask smart people questions, then just hang around and pick up information. I don't mean eavesdrop; I mean be around them and learn what they do by observing. Hope that some of their smart will rub off on you. Smart people have better conversations than stupid people. So figure out where smart, successful, rich people go and go there yourself. I doubt it will be a monster truck rally but you never know.

Here is the bottom line for getting smarter: The more information you have at your disposal, the better you are prepared in the decision-making process. When faced with a situation, you will have research you can fall back on that will help you make the best decision you can. Experience is a great teacher but a little solid research and education is hard to beat.

CHAPTER ELEVEN

MONEY RULES!

There are people who say money is overrated. Those people obviously don't have much of it. Having money is a lot better than not having money. If you've ever been in the position of not having any, you would know that. I like having it. I can do a lot of stuff with it I could never do without it. So don't ever diminish the importance of money or the joy of having it. If you do, you won't ever have much of it.

But money is a sensitive topic. Make too much and they say you can't be honest. Give away too much and people will question your motives. Place too much emphasis on it and folks will call you shallow. Place no emphasis on it and people (like me) will call you irresponsible. Place the wrong emphasis on it and you will have big problems!

I got in a discussion with some friends of mine recently over the topic of money. I commented about the people who write me and others in the "money" business about how we have become way too focused on money. Many write me to say that my books and some of the other books that are also very popular are more about greed than anything else. Can you believe what people will say? I actually do get these kinds of letters. It seems that when you tell people to be as successful as they can be and to earn as much money as they can earn, then you are considered greedy and money hungry. Tell people to live up to their potential and then get put down for doing it. Amazing, huh? These folks tell me they are offended by my constant focus on success.

I recently got a letter from a woman who told me it was more important for her to spend time with her kids than to be out "becoming more successful and rich." Holy crap! I will bet you this woman who talks about how important her kids are spends the bulk of her time sitting on her fat ass watching TV (maybe with them) and doesn't have a dime saved for their college education. Unfair? Maybe. She might be a wonderful mommy who really does spend time with her kids and if she is, I applaud her and apologize for my generalization.

But never shake your finger in my face telling me how altruistic you are and talk about how success isn't about money. Success is about money.

The Peace Corp—Habitat for Humanity—The Red Cross—The Salvation Army—the Susan G. Komen Foundation—United Way—and my personal charity of choice, Feed the Children—those charities and all the rest are about money. Money drives every charity. Money builds hospitals and homeless shelters. Money fights cancer. Money feeds hungry children.

That's why I work: to make money. Period. I recently gave a speech where the president of the company approached me when I was finished and said how lucky I was to be able to experience my passion like that. I asked him what he was talking about. He said, "Your speech. That is your passion, it's obvious." I said, "Thanks but that speech isn't my passion. That speech is my *job*. I am really good at my job and I'm glad you enjoyed me doing my job, but what you just witnessed is anything but my passion. I enjoy it but I'm not passionate about giving speeches." He was incredulous. I told him my passion was my wife, my boys, my bulldogs, and my free time. I told him I was passionate about sitting on my back patio with a glass of fine scotch in my left hand, a great cigar in my right hand, my bulldog on my lap, my wife by my side, watching the sun go down over the mountain while Merle Haggard plays in the background. That is something I can get passionate about. The rest is work. I do what I do for the money. I earn the money to pay for the life I love. I earn my money to finance as many nights sitting on my patio as I can get.

Why do you work? If it isn't for the money, you are a liar. Yes, you may find what you do extremely satisfying. You may even love it. But if the money wasn't there, you couldn't survive on satisfaction and love—you would need to go do something less satisfying that you didn't love so you could get paid. While I love what I do, if I didn't get paid well for doing it, I could fall in love with something else that did pay well.

I am tired of people pretending that money doesn't matter when it comes to work. It's the only thing that matters when it comes to work. And the way to make more money from your work is to be better at what you do. The better you serve others, the better others serve you . . . with their money. It all ties together: Service is tied to money. Charity is tied to money. Excellence is tied to money. Why does bringing money into the equation make it dirty for some people?

Money is the result of serving people well. Serving people is an honorable thing. Money is the result of hard work. Hard work is honorable. Having money is a wonderful thing in your life. It pays for college for your kids. It pays for healthcare when you and the people you love get sick. It takes care of your mom and dad when they get old and need help. It feeds the homeless and helps those who are less fortunate. It pays your taxes to build roads and provide fire and police protection. It's to be appreciated, saved, invested, and *enjoyed*.

Bottom line, money is important. If you don't think it's important, try going without it for a while. You won't last long. Want more of it? Work harder to serve others! Money is your reward for doing that.

MY STORY

You might think it strange that I have waited until the chapter on money to tell you my personal story. Most authors would have told you their story much earlier in their book in order to build their credibility and to give you a reason to keep reading. But my story is based on money so it's more appropriate for my story to come now. I began my whole journey of personal growth because of money—actually the lack of money. Everyone has a motivator. That motivator might be physical or mental abuse, weight, divorce, job loss, or any number of things. Mine was lack of cash.

While going to college, I worked as a telephone operator for Southwestern Bell Telephone Company in Muskogee, Oklahoma. After graduation I stayed with Bell, received several promotions, and was making a pretty good living—not a great living, but a pretty good living. Ten years later, several promotions later, and several cities later, I found myself in a position I no longer enjoyed and in a city I did not care for at all. Soon after the break-up of the Bell System, AT&T offered an early retirement package to many of the managers. I eagerly accepted, packed the truck, and headed back to Oklahoma. At that point I started my own telecommunications company selling business telephone systems. I had no seed capital and no knowledge of what it took to really run a business, but I did know how to sell telephones. So with a lot of hard work, determination, a dream, and the help of some good people, the company grew to become a real success. I started making good money and finally knew what it felt like to be a success financially.

Then, through a series of bad hiring decisions, misplaced trust in a few employees, a turn in the economy, my dissatisfaction with the telephone industry in general, my personal desire to do something else with my life, and a bunch of really stupid mistakes, my company went from being successful to a total disaster.

The company went into bankruptcy. As the company's founder and president, and the guy who had so eagerly put his name on all those dotted lines, I went into bankruptcy right along with it.

Sad story, right? Wrong. I earned that bankruptcy. I created it. I deserved it. I made it happen. The circumstances that led to it were the direct result of my actions. I take total responsibility. And while it was a horrible thing for me financially, it's still the single best thing that ever happened to me. I learned more as a result of that experience than I did in all of my years of education, and in all of my years of working in the corporate world. I learned lessons that have become the foundation of my speaking career. I learned it isn't what happens to you that matters; it's what you do about it that really matters. And I learned that being broke sucks!

I hated being broke. I hated having my car repossessed. I hated selling my stuff every weekend in a garage sale in order to have enough money to make my house payment and to make my child support payments and to be able to eat. (I was like the guy who sold everything he had except for his bicycle, and it didn't have a seat or any handlebars. He had lost his ass and didn't know which way to turn.)

That was the beginning of my journey, a journey that forced me to act immediately to change my financial situation. I didn't have time to wait for things to get better. I had to make them better right then. I also had to change the entire direction of my life if I were ever going to be truly financially secure. I had to study, since there were things I desperately needed to know. I had to change my habits. I needed to be willing to work harder than I had every worked before. I had to do whatever it took, regardless of how much I hated it in order to change my situation.

Which is exactly why you should listen to me when it comes to money. I grew up with not much money. I wasn't really what you would call "dirt poor" but I was dusty. I made the decision to get rich. I got rich. I lost it all and went bankrupt. I went from bankrupt to millionaire. Now I am a regular on many television news shows as a featured personal finance guru. I'm not really a guru, but I know some things that might help you out a bit.

Money Lessons

Making Money Unless you are a counterfeiter or the government, you don't *make* money. You *earn* money. Interesting how we forget that fact. We say, "I need to make some money!" Forget it. Instead of saying you need to make money, start asking yourself what service you can provide in order to earn more money.

Jim Rohn wisely taught that people make $5 an hour because they provide $5 worth of service and it takes them an hour to do it. People make $5,000 an hour because they provide $5,000 worth of service and it takes them an hour to do it. Why does one make so much more than the other? The difference isn't in the hour; the difference is in the amount of service you put in the hour.

We are all paid for service. But don't confuse service with working hard. You can work really hard and make very little. It isn't how much you sweat that increases your paycheck, although all of us could certainly afford to sweat a little more. I drive down my street and see men putting clay tile shingles on the top of a house in the middle of August in Arizona and the temperature is 115 degrees. They are working hard. I can see it. Yet I know they aren't getting rich doing it. Hard work makes you tired but it does not necessarily make you rich. Work that provides the most service to others makes you rich.

Make a list of all the ways you can add value to the lives of others: your customers, your boss, your family, your friends, even strangers. Begin now to think of your job in terms of service instead of just putting in the hours. Start focusing on the service and how you can continually add more value to everyone you work with. Do this and you will be amazed at how much better you feel about yourself, your job, and the people you serve. Plus, more money will show up.

Do More Than You Are Paid to Do. Soon you will be paid more for what you do. Some of you are balking at this one. That's probably why you don't have enough money. You hesitate to do one lick of work more than you absolutely have to. You do just enough to get by and then act surprised when someone else gets promoted. Are you kidding me? How can you be surprised when the people who do more, get more? Would you reward the person who not only did her job but went the extra mile? Of course you would. (By the way, the extra mile we have all heard about isn't very crowded—there's hardly anyone there at all.)

Get Your Attitude Right about Money. What is your attitude about money? You have a "money attitude" whether you are aware of it or not. You probably got your money attitude from your parents. It has been influenced by your social conditions, your ethnic background, your geographic area, your education, your age, and many other significant and sometimes not so seemingly significant events that all go together to become your personal historical experience in how you think about money. Some people refer to it as having a prosperity consciousness or a poverty consciousness. That sounds a little new-agey but it's pretty accurate.

A prosperity consciousness is based on your belief that there is more than enough for you and everyone else to be secure in all areas of life. All you have to do is be willing to do whatever it takes in order to make it happen. On the other hand, a poverty consciousness is based on a belief system of lack and limitation. It's buried in the fear that in order for someone to win, someone must lose. It believes that all abundance, including money, is limited. It also believes that no matter what you do, you will never have enough.

Whether you call it a consciousness of prosperity or poverty, your belief in abundance or lack is deeply rooted and has determined how much money you have. Your attitudes about money and about people who have money have determined exactly how much money you have this very minute.

"Make fun of the rich and you won't be one of us."

—Reverend Ike

So what is your attitude about money? Not sure? Look at how much money you have; that will tell you what you believe about money.

Here is an easy way to know how you feel about money: How do you feel when you spend it? And I don't mean when you are at the mall buying the things you can't afford to buy. I am talking about grocery shopping, making your insurance payments, paying your utility bills and your taxes, and giving to charity. Do you drag out paying your bills until the last minute just because you know you can get by with it? Do you grudgingly pay your taxes, griping every minute about how unfair it is? If you have a problem letting money go from you, then you will have a problem letting money come to you. Money comes to you as it goes from you.

10-10-10 Theory of Money

Save 10 percent. Invest 10 percent. Give 10 percent. Live on the 70 percent that's left. No way to argue with this one. It's simple math so it isn't hard to figure out the numbers. Any bozo can figure out 10 percent. And no one can argue with the fact that this will work for you. If you do this and have discipline and don't vary from it, you will achieve financial security. I could spend a lot of time on this one but come on . . . just do it. It's smart.

Save. Most folks simply don't have enough money saved to help them through any financial emergency and certainly aren't saving enough to retire.

Invest. I am not an investment advisor. I won't tell you where to put your money in order to make more money. But there are plenty of solid, trustworthy advisors who can tell you.

Give. It's not about being a religious tither. It's about being a good person. Be charitable. It's the right thing to do.

Live on less. Seventy percent of your income is enough to survive on if you are willing to cut back on your lifestyle to do it. Yes, it will require sacrifice. It will mean that you can't have every little thing your heart desires. But it can be done. Very few people can't live on less. The key is to learn to say no to yourself.

Spend Less Than You Make

I was recently interviewed on one of the news shows and a guy called in and asked me how I became one of the country's financial gurus. I told him I wasn't sure, since pretty much all I've got is "Spend less money than you make." But since 40 percent of people don't do that... I'm a guru!" Folks, it's very simple; you cannot be financially secure spending more money than you make. Don't complicate it much more than that. Cut back on your lifestyle and spend less money.

Simple Math

Good money management is just simple math. Write down how much money you to have to work with (your income). Write down how much money everything you have costs (your expenses). This includes your rent or mortgage, car payments, insurance, food, gas, utilities, and all of your other expenses. Then simply subtract your expenses from your income. You should have a positive number left. If you don't, you are spending more than you earn and you are an idiot. Fix it *now*. How? Two ways: Increase your income or reduce your expenses. It's that simple. "But I don't have the ability to make any more money!" Then your choices are pretty limited, aren't they? You have to reduce your expenses. Which means you are going to have to give up some things. Stop smoking. At $4 a pack, a one-pack-a-day habit is nearly $1,500 per year. Give up eating out, going out, your premium cable channels, and any number of frivolous items. Yes, those things are frivolous; they are not necessities. Funny how we now consider what used to be luxuries to be necessities. Rethink the way you live. You can live on less. You have no choice if you want to be financially secure.

Be Thankful for What You Already Have

"The first step toward discarding a scarcity mentality involves giving thanks for everything that you are and everything that you have."

—Dr. Wayne Dyer

"But I don't have much, what is there to be thankful for?"

Just give thanks for the way things are. It does not mean you are satisfied with things the way they are; it just means you are thankful things are not worse than they are. Does that help? I like what Zig Ziglar says, "The more you are thankful for what you have, the more you will have to be thankful for."

"But it's just terrible for me!"

That is okay, I have had it terrible before, too. I have been divorced, lonely, heartbroken, and bankrupt. I have allowed myself to be victimized by terrible guilt. I have hated my job, had money problems, had people close to me die, made some terrible decisions, embarrassed myself, said stupid, hurtful things to people I love, messed up in my marriage and with my kids and more. Does that really sound like my life is much different from yours? Or from anyone else's life, for that matter? I doubt it. The point is that terrible stuff happens to everyone. Everyone is an idiot from time to time. That is just the way it is. So it isn't special for people to have problems. What makes us special is that we can rise above our problems. It has been said so many times it has become a cliché: It isn't what happens to you that matters, it's what you do about it that matters.

Here is a good exercise for you. Yes, it involves making another list. But writing things down with a pen and paper has a tendency to put things in the proper perspective, so play along. Make a list right now of everything that is going right for you. Call it your "Things That Are Going Right for Me" list. Don't get too fancy. Just list the things that come to your mind quickly. Don't whine and say, "This is a waste of time because nothing is going right for me." Sure it is. You bought the book. So you had enough money to do that. Write that down: "I have enough money to buy a few good books." That probably means you have a job. Write that down. Even if it's a job you don't like and plan to leave, write down that you have a job—some people don't. Move forward. You are reading this book, so that means you have your eyesight. Write that down. You are not standing, are you? Then you have a chair. Write that down. You are not in the dark are you? Then you have electricity. Write that down.

"Stop! You have reduced this to the ridiculous."

Yes! I sure have. I just wanted to show you how easy it is to recognize things that are going right for you at some level. Life isn't a total disaster for you.

At this point feel free to scope up a little as you make your list. Include bigger things like your health. Or how about your car? Even if it's a clunker, write it down. It beats walking, right?

You are on your own now. Close the book and keep working on your list. When you finish, come back to this spot. Really. Close the book. Do the list. This book won't benefit you the way it was intended if you don't do the work I ask you to do. So close the book and make the list.

"When we hear somebody complaining that he has not enough, we may know that he has not expressed enough appreciation for what he already has."

—Lowell Fillmore

Study Money

Would you expect to be good at something if you didn't know anything about it? Probably not. Yet, it seems that people think they should automatically be good at handling money when they don't have a clue about it. I did a survey for my book, *Your Kids Are Your Own Fault*, asking my fan base what was the number one thing they wished their parents had taught them about. Ninety-nine percent (what I would call an overwhelming majority) replied with: MONEY.

It seems we aren't teaching people about money and that few really understand it. Look at the finances of most people; it's clear that most don't know much about money. Even the basics seem to elude most folks. In fact, one of the good things about tough economic times is that it wakes people up to their financial situation. It makes them, sometimes for the very first time, look at their income and expenses, their savings and their investments. It makes them aware of the economy in general and what a deficit and a surplus are. Bad times can do you a great service by waking you up and making you aware and forcing you out of desperation to study.

So what do you know about money? Most don't know too much. Most people barely know their financial situation. When I was shooting my A&E television series, "Big Spender," I was amazed that not one of the people had a clue how much money they had or how much they were spending. Then I found out that's pretty much the case with almost everyone. And it doesn't matter how many zeroes you have behind your income or expenses. The rich and poor alike are, for the most part, operating blind when it comes to their money.

Get a grip. Or as the saying goes, "You better check yourself before you wreck yourself!" Know that in all areas of life, there is information you need to know in order to do better. But if there was ever an area you needed to know more about, it's the area of money.

So what should you study? What books should you read? Selfishly, I would suggest you start with my #1 bestselling book, *You're Broke Because You Want to Be: How To Stop Getting By and Start Getting Ahead.*

Read some books about saving and investing. Read about budgeting. Watch some of the great financial shows on television. Some of them are really good. There are many great resources out there that can help you decide how to best take care of your money. Interview investment counselors. Find someone you trust who has a great track record with people in your similar situation. However, make sure this person has a lot more money than you do. Never trust your wealth to someone who does not have any. I get a lot of calls from brokers wanting me to do business with them, and I always ask how much money they make. They don't like that, but if they want my business, then they have to answer. If they don't make more than I do, there is no reason to do business with them. Never let a poor man tell you how to get rich. (That is a line you can highlight!)

Go to some seminars. Be careful here, though. If someone has a system for getting rich, make sure they are rich because of the system itself and not from just selling others the system. You don't really need much of a system. And you don't need to invest thousands of dollars with these get-rich-quick charlatans to figure out how to get out of debt and have a solid financial future. I will go way out on a limb here and say the investment involves reselling "opportunities," then run. And if their focus is more on recruiting than on their product or service, that is a clue! Very few make it in the network marketing business. Very, *very*, **very** few. And if any system you hear about involves the words "no money down," don't just run, run fast!

Bottom line: Learn more about money. Teach your kids about money.

Carry Heavy and Live Light

I always carry about $1,000 cash in my pocket. Why? It makes me feel better. Is it that I can't feel okay without all of that cash in my pocket? Of course not. I feel fine about myself with it or without it. I have plenty of confidence, but I still like the thousand bucks. When I am on stage giving one of my speeches and it's not going well (and believe it or not, that does happen from time to time), then I can always reach into my left pocket and feel that big wad of money and know it's okay if this particular speech isn't going all that well because I have a big wad of money in my pocket.

"But Larry, I certainly don't have a spare thousand dollars to be carrying around in my pocket!"

It doesn't have to be a thousand. Believe me, when I started this practice, it was not a thousand dollars. You can start this practice with any amount that makes you uncomfortable. Yes, I said uncomfortable. If it doesn't make you a little uncomfortable, then it won't make you feel ostentatious. And that is pretty much the point of the exercise. You have to feel a little cocky—not to the world—just to yourself. This is your own little prosperity consciousness confidence builder. I started with a $100 bill. Then I moved to a couple of them, then five, and up. You may have to start with a $20 or a $50. Which denomination you begin with isn't important, just put some cash in your pocket. A bit of excess cash in your pocket gives you some freedom. It allows you not to be burdened by the fact that lunch was more than you expected it to be. Or that you just ran across a great sale and you would really enjoy having that new pair of shoes. (Be careful with shopping with this money, however!) Besides, it's not about spending the money anyway. In fact, as soon as you spend it, you will need to replace it. It's about how it makes you feel when you're carrying it.

To me, carrying the money represents getting past being a broke little kid who grew up in Muskogee, Oklahoma, across the street from the Round-Up Club, who raised chickens and picked up pop bottles in order to have some spending money. It's a reminder of what I did to become who I am. It reminds me of the time when I was bankrupt and lost everything and what it took for me to come back from all of that. It represents freedom from my past. It's just a reminder of where I've been and where I never want to go back to. All of us need some reminders that we've been through some things. That pocket full of Benjamins is one of mine.

By the way, don't say to me you have a platinum card and there is no need for cash. You are so wrong. It simply isn't the same thing. Almost everyone has a platinum card—broke people have platinum cards. It's not about your buying power. It's about how cash makes you feel when you have some in your pocket.

Cash Is King

It always has been and always will be. Save some cash. Yes, put some in your bank account and save it. Investments are great. Rate of return is terrific. But don't worry so much about the rate of return being low that you use that as justification for not having some cash. Put some cash in a cigar box in a safe spot. Add to it whenever you can. Even if it's just a few dollars, that will add up over time. Be disciplined. Don't touch it until you have to. Leave it alone until a real need comes along. Think every day about how you can do without something in order to put away a few dollars in your cash box. Do without that Big Gulp or candy bar or that magazine. Hoard the cash instead.

Forget about the Economy

I'm talking about the national economy. A guy called in on a television call-in show I did recently. He said, "Larry, the Dow is off 185 points today, what do you think? Should we be concerned?" I asked him if he knew what the Dow even was. Answer; No. Then I asked if he had any money in the stock market. Again, No. So I responded, "Then what the hell difference does it make to you?" People get so caught up worrying about *the* economy that they don't take care of their own economy. Remember this: Control what you can control and let go of the things you can't control. You can't control the economy but you have total control over your own economy.

How Will I Know When I Have Enough Money? You can't measure your financial success in terms of an amount. No amount is ever enough. You are always going to want more money. You are going to want to get paid more, have more invested, and more saved. This will become more evident to you as you grow older and think about the fact you don't want to work until the day you die. The only way to know whether you are earning enough money, though, is when you have given your all and done your best. Only your best effort is enough.

Is $250,000 per year enough? Not if your full potential would be to make $2 million a year. If your best is in the millions and you make in the thousands, then you are not living up to the best you have to offer and not realizing your full potential.

Is $20,000 per year enough? It's plenty if you were paid that after giving the very best you have in the service of others. Have you served your best? When you went to work did you work every minute you were there and give it all you had? When you have done your best, given your best, and served the best you possibly can, then what you have received is the right amount.

What To Do When the Money Runs Out? I get a lot of e-mail from people who have either lost their jobs or are losing their jobs. Their 401K is gone, their savings account is zeroed out, or maybe their unemployment checks have run out. This is becoming a common situation for a good part of our society. Many people are facing a lack of employment and a lack of funds. Yet their family still needs to eat and the bills still have to be paid. Does this apply to you? I hope it doesn't. But I am betting that you know someone who is in this situation.

It's too late to tell people they should have saved more (six months cash set aside to cover your monthly expenses). It's too late to say you should have worked harder or smarter or better so you wouldn't have been the one who got laid off (not always the case but it's often the case). It's too late to say that you shouldn't have spent so much money on stupid stuff—that you shouldn't have wasted money on things that gave only very temporary satisfaction—that you shouldn't have gone out to eat four nights a week or bought that car you couldn't really afford or that house you knew you couldn't make the payments on if anything happened to your income. It's too late to beat people up about any of that stuff at this point, so I don't and I won't.

Instead, it's time to give folks some ideas they can use when it's crunch time, they are scrambling, and when survival is the main concern. So here are five things to do when the money runs out.

1. When it comes to looking for employment, get your ego out of the way. The fact is that your family needs food and your bills need to be paid. You have something called "commitments."

Which means you should be committed to paying them. You have "obligations." Which means you are obligated to pay them. When you got married, I am betting that your vows said something along the lines of "for richer, for poorer." That is the same vow you take with your other obligations and commitments as well. When you had your kids you didn't agree to make sure they had food only when you had the job of your dreams and times were good. You also didn't sign a contract with your mortgage company, bank, or credit card company saying you would only make your payments when you were employed. You just committed to taking care of your obligations. There were no conditions associated with your commitment.

I don't care that you used to be an engineer making $100 K per year. Now it's time to take a job where you say, "You want fries with that?" Or "Welcome to Wal-Mart, here's your basket." Or "Excuse me, I need to mop that spot right there." Or "I need to stop and get more gas for my mower." Or "Do you need a babysitter?" Get the point? You need to do whatever it takes to pay the bills and put food on the table and a roof over your kid's head simply because you said you would. You gave your word. It's the right thing to do.

There is no excuse not to do it. Sorry. Don't write me telling me some sad story. There is *no* excuse. I have sold plasma and mowed my neighbor's yard and swept floors and shoveled manure. I have sold scrap metal and cleared trash away. There was never anything I was too good to do when it came time to pay my bills or buy groceries for my family. Did I hate it? Every minute. Did I do it? Damn straight.

So do something. Anything. You aren't too good. It may not be your dream job. It may not be something you are proud of or can brag about or even want to tell anyone about. It probably won't be your new career. But if it feeds your family and pays your bills and is legal, do it.

2. Go into survival mode. Other financial gurus break things down into two categories: needs and wants. That doesn't go far enough in my opinion. I say that there is another category: Can't live without. How are you spending your money? Is it on things you want? Things you need? Or things you can't live without? If the money is running out or has run out, then the only things you can spend money on are the things you can't live without. What are those things? Food first. Shelter second. Commitments third. Nothing else gets your money.

3. Communicate. Call your creditors and explain your situation to them. Trust me when I say it won't be a new story they haven't heard before. Just tell them where you are and tell them what you realistically can do as far as paying them back. Remember that credit is judged on the willingness to pay and the ability to pay. Explain that you are high on willingness and low on ability. Of course this will have much more impact and credibility if your past payment history indicates that you are indeed high on willingness. Don't expect them to buy your story if you have habitually been a person who doesn't bother to make your payments on time. Regardless, you still need to make contact. You need to take the initiative. The key is to not hide out, dodge their calls, or ignore their letters. Talk to them and remember that it's their money that they fronted you based on you saying you would repay it and they have every right to want it back.

4. Sell. Go through your house and get rid of every single thing you can't live without. I sold my living room furniture and we sat on the floor. We needed to pay our house payment more than we needed a sofa. If you don't regularly use it, sell it. Start with your toys: golf clubs, boats, four-wheelers, motorcycles, bicycles, and all your other "toys." Then move to your closet, your DVDs, CDs, excess furniture, pictures, and anything else that isn't absolutely necessary to your survival. Be tough on yourself. It's amazing how little you really need to get by.

5. Know your new job. If you don't have a job, your new job is finding a job. Yep, finding a job *is* your job. My son, the fashion designer, lost his job. He had a little money saved up so he could last about three months before it hit the fan. He was sure he could find a new job in three months. However, at the end of three months, there was no new job and he was out of money. He did everything I suggested here. I visited him and he had practically no furniture left and very few clothes. He took on a roommate to help split expenses. He ate ramen noodles and boxed mac and cheese. But the most important thing was that he worked 12 hours a day searching for a job. He signed up on every online job search website (malakye. com, monster. com, and craigslist. com were a few). He put together resumes in the fashion industry as a designer, sample maker, pattern maker, and cutter and every other area where he could work in his area of expertise. He also had resumes that didn't say anything about fashion. Resumes that would work for any job: retail, sales, or sweeping floors. He slept with his BlackBerry in his hand and when a job posted in the middle of the night, his phone would buzz and he would immediately wake up and send the appropriate resume for that job posting so he could be one of the first responders to every job posting. He went on interviews all day long with anyone who would talk to him. He went on job interviews he knew he wouldn't get just to hone his interviewing skills. He interviewed for a forklift driver, janitor, door-to-door sales, and anything else that he could. He walked the streets, going into restaurants offering to wash dishes or bus tables. It was tough and he got depressed and was discouraged every day. But he kept at it. He finally found a guy with a bicycle shop who would let him work on bicycles and clean the place up. It wasn't even for minimum wage but it was still work. He still did everything he could every day to find something better. When he finally got an interview and an offer for a job as a fashion designer, it was for a quarter of the money he had been making. He took it. He worked his ass off and did whatever it took

to keep it. He knows how hard jobs are to come by and he knows what it's like to be broke. (For those of you who are saying, "Larry, why didn't you just bail him out?" Come on, you know me better than that. Besides, he didn't ask me to. He knew what it took and he did it. It was his job to figure out how to survive and to get another job.)

Here is my question for those of you who are in trouble: Are you doing whatever it takes? Have you done all five of my What To Do When the Money Runs Out? Or are you still waiting for your bailout package? It's not coming. Are you spending your time griping, bitching, whining, complaining, or blaming your employer, your creditors, or the government? That's stupid and a waste of time and energy. Besides, that only moves you farther from your goal, not closer. Your job is to do what it takes to survive, take care of your family, and pay your obligations. Go to work!

CHAPTER TWELVE

RELATIONSHIPS—FRIENDSHIP, MARRIAGE, AND OTHER CALAMITIES

Let me start by saying I am not an expert on relationships. However, I've read some of the books by people who claim to be experts and I have come to the conclusion they are not really experts either.

Most of the bestselling books on relationships point out that men and women are different—even from different planets. Do any of us really need a book to tell us men and women are different? That's sort of the basic attraction in the first place, in my opinion. It's not just that men and women are different; all of us are different. Again, no need for a book or a seminar on diversity to teach us that, just a little observation and common sense would do it. What we need to remember is that we are alike. It's the commonality we share that will bring us closer together, not the differences. We need to be discovering, nurturing, and celebrating what we have in common in order to have more harmonious relationships.

By the way, I don't really care who or what you are in a relationship with: male/female, female/female, male/male, young/old, person/farm animal or blow-up doll. I think that is your business and the rest of us should just butt out and leave you to it. As long as one of you isn't underage, then I don't care. Consenting adults have the right to pursue any relationship that is based in love and brings mutual happiness. Period. All of us need to keep our moralistic, hypocritical noses out of everyone's business and let people have some fun and find a love with which they feel comfortable. Bet I just lost a few of you right there, didn't I? That's okay—these ideas are meant to make you uncomfortable and force you to think in a whole new way. I did not say, "Force you to accept a whole new way of thinking." I said, "Force you to think in a whole new way." You can accept what you want to accept and what makes sense to you; I just want you to think a little. So it's okay if you have a problem with what I'm saying—let me finish, then think about it, see if it makes sense to you, use what you like, throw the rest away, and move on. Deal?

While there are many kinds of relationships, almost all of them rely on the same elements in order to succeed. Let's begin with friendship and then move on to marriage.

FRIENDSHIP

Friendship is just about the only relationship that exists entirely because you want it to. It isn't like family; you are stuck with those people no matter what. You cannot get rid of them even if you try. Everyone has a Cousin Eddie in the family (remember the *Vacation* movies?). Just duck your head and deal with it. You don't have a choice. But no one is forcing you to be friends. Friendship is always a choice.

You shouldn't have to work at friendship. Friendships should be easy. If you have to work to make it happen, then it really isn't a friendship—it's just someone you hang around with sometimes. Friends just accept you and let you be the way you are. They let you have your good days and your bad days. They allow you to be an idiot and make an ass of yourself. However, a friend will not let you whine. A real friend will kick your butt and force you to take responsibility.

You don't need too many friends. That has never really been a problem for me. I have never had very many. It isn't easy being my friend—I am what you call "hard to get along with." So when someone is my friend, it's because they really want to be. I appreciate that. I love my friends. I will do what it takes to help them. Period. No judgment. No questions asked. I think that is what being a friend is all about. And it should come easily.

Some people say marriages are like that. They say you should not have to work at marriage; it should be easy like friendship. I disagree. My wife and I never work at our friendship. We work at our marriage every day. Our marriage is sometimes a wreck. Our friendship is always intact.

It's probably better to have a good friend than it is to have a good spouse. But if you can get them both in the same person, you are truly blessed. So get a good friend and relax. Get a good spouse and go to work.

MARRIAGE

Source: Larry Winget, "Shut Up, Stop Whining, and Get a Life," SmarterComics.

The failed marriage statistics are staggering in this country. Half of all marriages don't work and end in divorce. A bad thing? Not necessarily. Marriage isn't the end-all/be-all of living a fulfilled life. It's not for everyone. Yet society has implied that in order to be fulfilled, we must be married. That could not be more wrong. I'm not surprised most marriages end in divorce. We have a totally screwed up view of marriage that pretty much dooms it from the start.

We often think marriage provides us with stability. There isn't any real stability in marriage. Marriage is like everything else: It's made up of constantly changing organisms that expand, contract, move, grow, and die. These changing organisms, when combined into a relationship, are responsible for the shape and makeup of the marriage. People change, therefore relationships between people must change. That is just life at its most basic level. Things change. It's natural.

Don't think I have a bad view of marriage. I don't. I love being married. I am only being realistic about the institution that binds two people together for what some people believe should be forever, even if the two are miserable and hate each other. That's just dumb. People grow. Sometimes people grow at different rates and in different directions, and they end up growing apart. There are other times when people just lose interest in doing the work it takes to maintain a good relationship. There are also times where people become interested in someone else.

This is just reality. The key is to understand that every situation, including marriage, is temporary. You may be saying, "Not my marriage." Well, then you are naive. The only way to have a happy marriage is to have one that is happy moment by moment. You can plan to be happy 20 years from now with your current relationship, but you may end up severely disappointed.

The best relationships and marriages renew themselves constantly. They don't focus too much on the future. They don't put much stock in the past. Instead, they focus on the right now.

They put their energy into enjoying every second of what they have at that moment.

Is all of this blasphemous to the marriage vows? I hope so. The marriage vows need to be blasphemed. They are based in the ancient laws of ownership, when women were no better than chattel, except they could bear the children and cook the food.

Marriage is a social contract that imposes fear, guilt, obligation, and compromises individuality. Fear and love can't exist at the same time. Guilt serves no purpose but to destroy. Obligation breeds resentment. Compromised individuality is the loss of self.

"The trouble with wedlock is, there's not enough wed and too much lock."

—Christopher Morley

I have other issues with the institution of marriage and its abuses.

Who or What Are You Really Committed to?

Many people are much more committed to their marriage than they are to their spouse. Many people are so committed to the institution of marriage that they stay in unhappy, abusive marriages rather than divorce.

If you doubt that, just look around. Do you know couples who are miserable with each other? Do you know people who literally can't stand each other, yet because they are married, wouldn't think about changing their situation? Is that your definition of a marriage? Not mine.

In many cases, couples are so committed to their children that they stay together under horrible circumstances. Children never benefit from being raised in a house where love is absent between the parents. In those situations, parents only set an example of a loveless home for their children to use as a role model. They later wonder why their kids have lousy marriages, asking themselves in their best woe-is-me voice, "Where did I go wrong?" Where did you go wrong? You gave them a bad example as a role model.

I could walk away from my marriage tomorrow and wouldn't feel a thing. Really. Never look back and smile the entire time. In fact, many times I have been very tempted to do just that. Yet I could not walk away from the person I am married to.

Some of you are thinking I am a total creep right now for saying that about my marriage. But before you judge, look carefully at what I am saying.

I have no commitment to the institution of marriage. However, I have a total commitment to the person I am married to. Which is better? I know my wife prefers the personal commitment rather than the institutional one. She enjoys the institutional one but given a choice would take the personal commitment anytime. I bet you and your spouse would pick the same way if you stopped to consider it.

Taking Each Other for Granted

For many people being married is like being tenured in your job. You let your behavior slide because there is no risk of losing your job anyway. I'm not a fan of tenure—not for teachers and not for any relationship. I believe tenure is a license for laziness. And a tenured marriage is doomed. The moment you take anything for granted in a relationship, whether it be with your employer, your friend, or your spouse, you start getting lazy. Think of your friends. Know the couple who used to be college sweethearts? She was the cute little cheerleader and he was the BMOC jock. Twenty years later, she's still cute and trim and takes care of herself and he has a belly that covers his belt buckle because he's 50 pounds overweight. He takes his wife for granted. He says he loves her and he probably does. He just doesn't love her enough to maintain his health or his looks because he thinks the relationship is golden regardless. Comedians use this as a joke all the time: "Why should I care about my looks? I'm married." Ladies, you aren't getting off on this one, though. I often see guys who work hard at staying fit even though they work hard all day and do the daddy thing along with all of their other commitments. They look good. Then you see their wife and say to yourself, "Really?" She's dumpy, gray roots, and has gotten to the point where she thinks a clean pair of sweats is dressing up. Then she can't understand why her husband cranes his neck at the mall when a hottie walks by. It's not like his wife is giving him anything interesting to look at. Shallow? Yeah, but people are shallow. And they are visual. And this is evidence that couples take each other for granted, both men and women.

It isn't just looks, though. When you were dating, did you open the door for your wife? Then you still need to be doing it. When you were dating and first married, did you greet him in the morning with a cup of coffee while he shaved for work? Then you still need to be doing it. Did you rub her feet after a hard day? Then you still need to be rubbing her feet. Did you compliment each other? Then do it now. Did you talk about the other's day, or their dreams, or desires, or fantasies? Then you better do it again. If you don't do these things—and believe me, this is a skimpy list used only for example—then you are lazy and taking your spouse and your relationship for granted.

Marriage Creates Possessiveness

The marriage certificate isn't a bill of sale; it isn't even a rental agreement. However, some people look at marriage like a certificate of ownership, saying in essence, "It's mine and I can do whatever I want with it." Legally, you are correct. You can do whatever you want with your relationship because it's yours.

It's much like buying a house; you can buy a house, never clean it, never spray for termites, never paint it, never take out the trash, and let it build up in the kitchen until it stinks and attracts bugs and mice and other varmints. You can do that to your house because it's yours. You own it. Not much can be done about it if that is the way you choose to treat your possession. But just because you can do it, doesn't make it a good idea.

You can buy a new car, never clean it, park too close to people and get dings on the side, never change the oil, and drive on bald tires. It's yours; you own it and you can do whatever you want with it. But is it a good idea? I don't think so.

Ownership creates two kinds of people: those who have pride in ownership, even to the point of obsession, and those who immediately say, "It's mine and I'll do what I damn well please with it."

Marriage works the same way. I suggest you become one of those obsessive people, constantly tending to the relationship in order to leave it better than when you first got it.

Look good for each other. Dress up for each other. Clean up before bed. Women, wear your makeup to bed sometimes and men, splash on some of her favorite cologne before you hit the sheets. Do the stuff you did to seduce each other in the beginning. Put in the effort it takes to keep the spark going. I got some interesting reviews on this book when it first came out regarding these last suggestions. Some women claimed that they were too busy to put on makeup and look good for their spouse because they had kids and homework and laundry and a whole list of excuses why they couldn't be bothered with their appearance. Okay, fine. Be too busy. Just don't be surprised when your husband loses interest because you can't find the time. Don't you dare whine to your friends, "I have no idea what happened!" Same for you guys. I know you are tired and I know you are busy. Suck it up and take care of yourself even when you don't feel like it.

Marriage Is a Romantic Myth

Don't accuse me of being some unromantic jerk. I'm not. All of us just need to take some of the romance out of marriage for a moment and look at it more realistically. Marriage is made up of two individuals who choose to live together happily for as long as they possibly can. Marriage must be a choice, not an obligation.

Please don't misunderstand me here. I am all for romance. But romance has to do with the quality of the relationship, not about the contract of marriage. We have romanticized marriage to the point we think it's the only way to live happily together.

And my wife and I do love each other. Very much. But we also have times we aren't that wild about each other too. Don't you? If not, you are lying to yourself and the rest of us.

"How do you feel about living together before marriage, Larry?" I'm for it. You don't know someone until you live with them. I'll even go so far as to say that I believe we should make it a federal law that two people can't marry until they have lived with each other for a period of one year. Smell each other, see each other at your worst, pick up after each other, learn everything that is wrong with the other person. Their good moods and their lousy moods. After a year, either walk away with no obligations to each other or get a marriage license. If this law were passed I guarantee we would cut the number of divorces by half. There is no way you can ever know anyone until you live with them.

"Wouldn't that be living in sin?" I love moralistic judgment, don't you?

It depends on your definition of sin. I think the real sin is allowing people to get married when they don't really know the person they are marrying. And if you are now married or have been married, then you know you did not know the person you married until you lived together for at least a year. As Will Rogers said, "It doesn't much signify who one marries, for one is sure to find out the next morning it was someone else."

The marriage myth is that we will be joined together in perfect harmony: two halves finally being united to make a whole. What a misguided, romanticized load of crap. Two people are being joined together in the myth that if only they had a joint checking account and shared a last name, they would be happy.

We must learn to be strong, independent individuals perfectly capable of being alone and enjoying it before we even consider joining together with another person in a legally binding contract that when ended will leave at least one of the participants in financial ruin.

"So are you against marriage?"

No.

"Are you for divorce?"

Yes.

There is nothing wrong with divorce. Get off your high horse on this one, since 50 percent of all marriages end up that way anyway. More people should get one. Divorce is the correct solution to many crummy marriages. (So is counseling and therapy, by the way.) I believe we would have fewer divorces, though, if we reexamined marriage. I believe if we had strong individuals entering into marriage, divorce rates would go way down.

I would much rather see a couple divorce in order to find true love with another person, or even to live happily alone, than to stay in a relationship that is destructive emotionally, mentally, or physically.

> **It's better to have a good divorce than a bad marriage.**

Individuality

In any relationship, you must maintain individuality. Most relationships rob people of their individuality. It takes two people and turns them into one entity. Relationships force us into the role of being two halves instead of two wholes who meet to enjoy their wholeness.

When we enter into a relationship with another person we become a couple. In many cases that is exactly what we become: a couple of weak little people struggling to discover who we are through the life of another person.

We somehow lose ourselves into that dark abyss of pronouns called "they, them, we, and us." It's interesting how we are no longer ourselves to the rest of the world because now we are a couple. Some would say, "How sweet." I say, "How sickening." It's this very type of thinking that ruins many lives. We lose who we really are to become who *they* are.

Many couples become linked like conjoined twins—usually at the head. It seems once we are in a relationship we can no longer think without the aid of the other person. We suddenly can't decide what to wear or what we look good in. We can't figure out what type of music we like, what food we like to eat, where we like to go, what we like to do, and if we have time to do it without checking with our " other half " or "better half " first.

What happened to us? We gave up our individuality. We entered into the relationship to find ourselves only to end up losing ourselves instead. We are not ourselves anymore; we are "us."

Then something happens to "us." Any number of things. And suddenly, we don't know who we are any longer. Is it any wonder? You sold yourself out when you became us. You lost your identity. You lost what made you, you. Sad. Pitiful, really.

The solution? Maintain your individuality. Develop yourself as an individual. Keep your own interest. Do things by yourself. Do things that have nothing to do with your spouse or partner. Stay you! Do this knowing that the better you are for yourself, the better the two of you will be.

I was once flying out of Las Vegas and seated next to a very old couple. She was seated at the window, he was in the middle, and I had the aisle seat. I was writing some thoughts for this book on my laptop and had just typed the line, "A good divorce is better than a bad marriage." He was evidently reading what I was writing, and leaned over to me and said, "You got that right!" He then went on to introduce themselves as G. R. and Ethel Griffin and told me they had been married for 62 years. Isn't that amazing? They had just spent the week in Las Vegas gambling and seeing shows and eating out. They were truly a hoot to talk to. I finally asked them their secret for staying married for that long. She jumped in and said, "I'll take this one." (Which might be the secret right there!) Then she added, "Just let the other person be who they are and put up with it." That just may be the best marriage counseling anyone could ever receive. She told me that after 62 years together they both still had plenty of things they didn't like about each other, but they cared enough about each other to just put up with it. Whole books about relationships and how to have a great marriage have been written with less said than Ethel did in that one sentence. By the way, I have used that line as a toast at many weddings—feel free to use it too, but give Ethel credit if you can remember to.

We all have these ideas about how we want the other person to be. Chances are, it's not going to happen. People are rarely who we want them to be. (A fact that has bothered me a good number of times in my married life.) People are who they are. Period. No more. No less. Shut up, stop whining, and put up with it.

Someone asked me recently what I loved most about my wife, Rose Mary. Good question, huh? How would you answer that one about your spouse? It was an easy answer for me.

What I love most about Rose Mary is that she loves me. Believe it or not, that isn't an easy thing to do and most people either couldn't or wouldn't do it. I am almost impossible. I am loud. Obnoxious. Intolerant. Demanding. Caustic. Sarcastic. Impatient.

A perfectionist. A neat freak. And those are my good traits. In fact, I have often said that the real key to our long relationship is the fact that we are both in love with the same man. Go ahead and laugh, it's funny. By the way, I said that the other day on Facebook and someone said, "I know which man Larry means when he says that: Jesus." Sorry folks, I meant me.

Rose Mary loves me just the way I am. Regardless. Yes, she would love me if there were things about me that were different. She could do without my sarcasm and caustic style and sometimes wishes I would dress like a normal guy. But she puts up with it.

Opposites Attract but Not for Long

Source: Larry Winget, "Shut Up, Stop Whining, and Get a Life," SmarterComics.

We've been told that opposites attract. In magnets maybe that is a good thing, but in relationships not so much. Where people are concerned, opposites attract but not for long. You simply must have things in common—lots of things. Otherwise you will tire of each other, find each other boring, and begin to resent each other for not sharing common interests.

I think that is why so many people divorce after their kids leave home. Once the kids are gone, they are faced with only each other. Up until that point, their only common interest was the children, but now what is left? In most cases, not much.

"Whatever your woman is into, you better be into. Whatever your man is into, you better be into. Your partner into church, you better be into church. Your man or woman a crackhead, you better be a crackhead. Otherwise it just won't work."

—Chris Rock

We have all seen couples where both people are totally different, but if their relationship is a good one, I guarantee it's because they have plenty of things in common that the rest of us don't see. My wife and I amaze people because we are so totally different. She is sweet, nice, conversational, a peacemaker, and everyone who meets her adores her. On the other hand, I am none of those things. In fact, I am everything she isn't and she is everything I am not. But other than our personalities, we are very much alike. We both love the same architecture, the same movies, going to restaurants, shopping, travel, books, the same kind of people, decorating, cooking—just about everything she likes to do, I like to do, and the other way around. That's what makes it work for us. We share 80 percent of the same likes and dislikes. However, we have very different personalities.

And while it's very important to have things in common, few couples have everything in common. True compatibility is just too much to expect and mostly overrated in my opinion—even though we have made it grounds for divorce: "We are incompatible, Your Honor, give us a divorce." Better yet are irreconcilable differences. I have yet to see any two people who are totally compatible. And every relationship is full of irreconcilable differences. Few relationships hit on all cylinders. There is always something. One wants sex all the time and one is just not that interested. One loves to travel and the other is a homebody. One loves mornings and the other is a night owl. One loves social events and the other is a recluse. One loves antiques and the other likes contemporary. You get the drill. Think of your own relationship. Are you really compatible in all areas? I doubt it. Do you and your partner have differences that are irreconcilable? I bet you do.

Does it really matter? Not totally. It's okay to be completely different in some areas. In fact, it's to be expected. Not too different in too many areas, but some. It makes it interesting. However, the sex one will be a problem for you if that is the area of incompatibility. A person either has their needs met at home or they will have them met elsewhere. If you don't romance your partner, she will find someone who will. If you don't talk to your partner, he will find someone who will. If you don't have sex with your partner, he will find someone who will. I promise. This is how it works whether you want to admit it or agree with it or not. Everyone does what it takes to get their needs met, regardless of what those needs are. And if a person doesn't get her needs met somewhere, she will lead a life of frustration and resentment. But other than sexual incompatibility, the rest is just window dressing.

My wife loves getting up early in the morning. Her eyes and mouth open at the same time. She wants to hop out of bed and run off with a big smile on her face to fix a healthy breakfast while watching the sun come up. She loves hearing the birds sing and enjoys making the coffee and spending an hour with the newspaper. Then she wants to exercise.

I want to wake up about nine, stumble in to get a big hot cup of coffee, watch a little television, and then about 10:30 or 11 go face down in a plate of bacon and eggs. I do eventually get around to the exercise part but it's going to be much later in the day.

My wife is also a vegetarian. And she doesn't eat anything fried. I know, boring, huh? My favorite food is chicken-fried steak and fried okra. And this is just the beginning of the differences we have.

Are those differences between us ever going to change? I can promise they are not. Those differences are absolutely irreconcilable. We are totally incompatible in those areas and many more.

But is it grounds for divorce? I can assure you it isn't. Our differences can be annoying as hell, but they aren't a reason to dump the marriage.

So what is my point? Scope up. So you do things differently. So you don't like many of the same things. So there are areas of life where you drive each other absolutely crazy. Get over it. Remember the advice, "Let the other person be who they are and put up with it!"

Discover the differences between each other and enjoy them. Make them a source of humor instead of a source of irritation. My whole family makes fun of me for sleeping late. Do I care? Not a bit. I laugh it off while I roll over, cover up my head, and squeeze in another 30 minutes of snoozing. We also tease my wife about her seeing the sun come up. A total waste of sleep time, in my opinion. I saw the sun come up once. I have a good memory and don't need to see it again. And as for the birds, I usually end up flipping the bird instead of hearing one sing.

Scope up! We are all different. That's part of what makes it fun. That's what makes it interesting. That's what keeps it from being boring.

When my wife and I married, I didn't have all that much to offer her. But I made her this promise, "It will never be boring." So far, I've kept my word.

You Don't Need Anyone

Give me a minute here before you totally dismiss me as an idiot and write off this statement. I spent much of my life as a needy person. I needed to feel loved, appreciated, and adored. This was a fear-based belief that was grounded in my own insecurities. As a result of being so needy, I created an environment that fed my insecurities.

I wanted the complete attention of my wife. I got it. I demanded her time, her focus, her adoration, her energy, and her presence. I felt better.

I did the same with my sons. My sons lived with their mother, my first wife. I felt guilty about not having them with me and I became needy to make sure they loved me. I never cut them any slack on visitation so they could have time for their friends or for their own life. It was time awarded me by the court—I had paid for it, I deserved it, I wanted it, I took it.

I also created a similar atmosphere in my speaking business. I needed the appreciation of an adoring crowd. I gave my audiences exactly what they said they wanted. I certainly was not giving them what I wanted to give them.

This need was very destructive. It nearly destroyed my marriage. It caused problems with my sons. And it made me disgusted with myself because I was selling out to my audiences.

Over a period of time, I realized this approach was not working well for me. No one was happy—not my family and not me. I finally realized that my happiness didn't have to rely on others feeding my ego. I started taking responsibility for my happiness and began to deal with my insecurities. My personal development took me past the point where I needed the approval of others. I had something more important: my own approval. Personal satisfaction comes only when you rise above the need for approval from others.

It first came with my audiences. I stopped telling them what they wanted to hear and started saying what I wanted to say. I started talking about things that were important to me and stopped caring about what they thought of me as a person. If they didn't like it, oh well, I probably wasn't coming back anyway, so it didn't matter. I became detached from my need for audience approval. I didn't care whether they gave me a standing ovation, a sitting ovation, or any ovation. I didn't care whether they bought my books, audios, and videos when the speech was over. I stopped giving the speech the people who hired me wanted me to give and started giving the speech I knew I needed to give. I held firmly to the belief that if I said what I wanted to say and believed in, the right audiences would show up. Know what? They did. I got more business than ever. Why? They believed me. They knew I believed in what I was saying. I discovered most people don't believe what you have to say—very few will even listen to what you say—but people will eagerly listen and pay to find out if you believe what you have to say. The audiences could tell I believed in my message of personal responsibility and service to others. Audience approval went up. Bookings increased. Fees increased. Why? Because I was willing to release my need for approval. And I became authentic. Authenticity in any field is always rewarded.

However, the reaction of many of my peers in the personal development industry wasn't positive. Many thought that my detachment from the audience was inconsiderate to them. They didn't understand the meaning of detachment. Detachment doesn't mean you don't care; it means you give up the need to control the results. I do care about my audiences. I care enough to give them the very best I have to offer: me. The real me. And the criticism I receive from others in the business—well, who gives a rat's ass anyway? Are they hiring me? No. Not one other person who is in the business ever wrote me a check to come speak for them.

The biggest challenge when it came to detachment for me was with my spouse. How can you accept the idea that you no longer need your spouse? It was one of the hardest things I ever did—the most painful withdrawal I ever experienced. Yet, in my opinion, it was absolutely necessary for happiness.

My need for her approval, presence, and adoration absolutely strangled our relationship. Destroyed it really. I took everything she had. I stole her from herself. I completely used her up. Then the day came when I grew to the point that I no longer needed her approval, and what was she left with? Nothing. How unfair of me. Most people thought we had the perfect relationship. Far from it. Appearances can fool you. We were so close, but not close for the right reasons. Close out of need, not out of want. It's much more important to want to be with someone rather than to need to be with someone. Need is based in lack and fear—want is based in desire. We all want to be wanted, but few really want to be needed.

However, that's rarely how it works. People come together thinking two halves make a whole. I know I keep saying that, but it has become so much a part of how we think that it needs to be attacked at every level, time and again. Only two whole people can make a whole relationship. Two people who view themselves as half of a relationship are doomed, because sometimes the halves do not line up. Few people, though, are strong enough to stand alone—confident and whole—next to another strong, confident whole person and create a healthy relationship. Instead, most relationships are based on two emotional cripples joined at the hip pretending they have created one whole, successful being. Wrong.

In the movies we hear the line "You complete me." From Austin Powers and Mini-Me all the way to Tom Cruise. Similar lines have become popular in many movies where the audience swoons when they are said. It has become popular to need someone to the point that only her presence makes us whole. That is just sad and pitiful. No one completes you. In fact, my plan is to write a relationship book called, "You Do NOT Complete Me." Nothing outside of yourself completes you. As soon as we realize we are already complete and always have been, the better off we will be.

"The purpose of relationships is not to have another complete you. But to have another with whom to share your completeness."

—Neale Donald Walsch

The Great Dichotomy. Okay, let me really confuse the issue. I have just said that you don't need anyone; no other person can really make you happy. All true. However, you can't be happy without others, either. That is the great dichotomy of life: You don't need others to be happy and yet you can't be happy without them. Is it any wonder we have so many issues? Nothing is clear when it comes to relationships!

No one succeeds alone. No one is truly happy alone. We need each other. We were given to each other to love, to play with, to argue with, to enjoy. That means we have to figure out how to get along with each other. A challenge for sure—one I have yet to completely figure out. But I do have some solid ideas I know will work for you.

Forgiveness

Relationships are full of offenses. And marriage probably has more than most other relationships. Two individuals attempting to get along with each other in continuous harmony is almost a ridiculous idea to begin with, don't you think? Anger, hurt feelings, resentment, arguments, unkind words—to think there won't be all of those things and much, much more is just stupid. I know you've been told that the key to dealing with offenses is to forgive and forget. How's that working for you? Doesn't work that well for me. When I was able to forgive, I never forgot, which probably just meant I never really forgave in the first place.

I'm just not good at forgiving. I don't honestly think many of us are. I like my grudges; I like to wallow in the misdeeds of others. Not very enlightened, huh? And certainly in contradiction with much I have said here in this book. But still honest.

Forgiveness is hard. Especially when you have really been "done wrong."

A Stupid Promise.   My wife and I are not on our first marriages. Sometimes it takes one marriage to figure out what you are not willing to live with before you end up getting it right. Does it have to be that way? I don't know, but second marriages seem to last longer than first marriages according to the stats. It seems you aren't as idealistic the second time around. Usually it's because people just get married too young. Look at the 21-year-olds you know. Would you trust a person that age to make a life-long decision for you? And some kids get married earlier than that! It takes a little living before someone is able to make a life-long decision when it comes to choosing a life-long mate.

When Rose Mary and I got married, I had the words "I'll always take care of you" etched into the inside of her wedding band. Romantic, huh? Then after 15 years of marriage I messed up. Amazing I'm willing to admit it, isn't it? I know many of you will accuse me of adultery, promiscuity, of being a sinner, and any number of things you can conjure up in your mind. In fact, many have written terrible things calling both me and my wife names in their book reviews of this book. That's fine; think what you want and say what makes you feel better. However, I don't really care what you think of me. I didn't do what I did to you. I did it to Rose Mary. What did I do and why did I do it? None of your business. I don't owe you an explanation of my transgression. I am willing to share it in order to be honest about who I am and to teach you a lesson I had to learn the hard way. Bottom line is, though, it happened. And in the process, I broke the promise I had inscribed inside her wedding ring and I stopped taking care of her.

We got past it. Barely. It was horrible. We got a good counselor and put our marriage back together. It took years. We cried. We screamed. At times, we hated each other. But we eventually agreed that we loved each other too much to give up on our relationship, so we stuck it out.

When things were not going well for us, she took off her ring and put it in a drawer. She just didn't believe me anymore and I couldn't blame her. I had broken the trust we had between us. She had discovered the hard way that I was not going to "always take care of her" as her wedding ring promised.

As a result, a major revelation happened for both of us. No one can take care of you other than yourself. You are responsible for your happiness. No one else can do it for you. Stop relying on any other person to take care of you and learn to take care of yourself.

As we proceeded through our counseling sessions it became apparent we had a real chance of salvaging our marriage. Even though she hated what I did, we loved each other enough to work it out. At the turning point in our counseling, I took her ring from the drawer where she had been storing it and took it to the jeweler where I had the lie removed from the inside of the ring. It would no longer say, "I'll always take care of you." This statement we both had learned was both unrealistic and impossible. I had it replaced with "Love. Honor. Respect." What more can any person ask from any other person? Marriage, friendship, parenting, family, co-workers, strangers—you name it—any time people, countries, organizations, or entities of any type come together those three words should be the basis of the relationship.

I love you enough to want the best for you and to give you my very best in all our dealings.

I honor you enough to be honest with you, to share my time with you, and to make myself vulnerable to you by sharing the best of who I am with you.

I respect you enough to hold you in the highest esteem to others, never degrading who you are or what we have together.

Forgiveness Isn't Easy. As I have just admitted, I messed up in my marriage. I've messed up a lot of things in my life but this is the one that matters the most. In the midst of my wife's anger, sadness, and hurt—she messed up and hurt me, too. No details here either and keep your judgment to yourself. Now we were both hurt. But this was different. I had been done wrong and I was pissed! There was no way I was going to forgive her. I had cried and begged for her forgiveness and she gave it to me, but now I couldn't bring myself to do the same for her. She had forgiven me of my wrongs so why could I not forgive her?

I don't know why, I just couldn't. I hated what had happened to me. I hated her for doing it to me. Yes, I loved her, but I hated her too. And I couldn't get over it. I tried. I read several books on forgiveness. I had even written and talked about it in some of my other works. It was very easy for me to tell others about the freedom that comes through forgiveness. And while I could counsel others on it, I would have nothing to do with real forgiveness when it came to her. That stuff was for those who had not been wronged as I had been wronged. Their problems were trivial; mine was personal! It's amazing what hypocrites we can all become when it gets personal.

So while my wife and I stayed together and did our best to make it work, it was not working. I brought up her mistake on a regular basis in order to make her feel bad. I did my best to hurt her over and over again by reminding her how wrong she had been and how she had hurt me. I justified every bad thing I was doing to her by comparing it to what she had done to me. In summary, my inability to forgive her was tearing us apart.

But even more than that, it was tearing me apart. There is no way to be happy in a relationship when you harbor anger, resentment, and unforgiveness toward the other person.

The problem was, I didn't feel she deserved forgiveness. Yes, she had apologized and I knew she was genuinely sorry. She did everything a human being could be expected to do to let me know she had messed up and felt horrible for it. But it still was not enough for me. I wanted more. I wanted her to deserve forgiveness.

Finally, while reading a little book called *The Four Agreements* by Miguel Ruiz, I read a line that said sometimes the offending party really doesn't deserve forgiveness. He pointed out you don't forgive others because they deserve it; you forgive others because you deserve it.

Bingo! That was it for me. I have always believed I deserved the very best in life. I have convinced myself of it completely. However, here I was in a relationship with a woman I genuinely loved and adored and yet I was miserable— all because I could not forgive her. Plus, I was making her miserable and ruining our life together in the process, all because I was waiting for her to do something that was beyond her power. I was waiting for her to earn my forgiveness—to deserve it. I suddenly realized that was never going to happen. Yes, everyone deserves forgiveness. Everyone. No matter what our transgression, all of us deserve forgiveness. But as humans, our humanness sometimes won't allow it.

A great song by Lyle Lovett talks about his girlfriend doing him wrong and he says that God will forgive her. Then the song says, "God will, but I won't and that's the difference between God and me."

As humans we must deal with the ego. My ego—my humanness—wouldn't let me forgive her. At least not because she deserved it. But I deserved it. And that was the release I needed. I forgave her because I deserved to be free of the sadness and anger and resentment. I deserved a happy, relaxed, loving relationship again. And the only way to get there was to let go of my unforgiveness. So I did. I forgave her. Not because I thought she deserved it. I forgave her because I desperately needed to move on.

Do you have people in your life who have "done you wrong?" If you are like most people, then you do. Are you harboring anger, resentment, and hard feelings toward them? Let it go. Forgive them. Not because they deserve it—because they honestly may not. But do it because you deserve it.

Easy? Absolutely not. Necessary? Absolutely.

Freedom

Most folks think that relationships, especially marriage, are based on a commitment and that commitment takes away your freedom. A paradox: commitment and freedom. Can you have both? Yes.

In fact, you can't have one without the other. Freedom is a necessity in order to have a strong commitment.

The Freedom to Enjoy Aloneness. We all need time for ourselves. Time to do the things we like to do without fear of taking away time from the other person. Men need to be able to hang out with their guy friends without fear of repercussion from their wife or girlfriend. Women need to do the very same thing. Luckily, in my life this isn't a big problem. I travel a lot so I get time to be alone. Sometimes I really enjoy room service, a stupid movie and no wife, dog, or cat around to bother me. I enjoy turning off the cell phone and isolating myself from the rest of my world for a few hours. Does that make me a selfish person who doesn't appreciate his wife, dog, or cat? No. It means I enjoy time for me—just me. My wife likes to go to wine tastings and to hang with her friends talking about stuff I don't give a hoot about. I don't do chitchat and I don't want to taste wine—I want to drink it. I like to stroll through mega-sporting goods stores. She likes wine stores. Sometimes she goes alone and has a fabulous time. She doesn't want me there, she doesn't need me there, and she likes doing this all by herself. She likes to get up early and read the paper. I like to stay up late and watch TV. When I wake up earlier than usual, it interrupts her alone time and she isn't particularly happy with me. When she decides to stay up late and watch TV with me, it's not always my favorite thing. Those are times that belong to us as individuals, not as a couple. We do lots of things as a couple but we also enjoy our time alone. We encourage each other to explore things the other can do alone. This is healthy for all relationships. Individuals must have time for themselves. I know a couple that is so insecure that they never let the other do anything alone. She demands that he spend all of his days off with her and makes him feel horrible when he wants to spend time with the guys going camping, shooting guns, or going out for a beer. So the guilt comes out "Why don't you want to spend your time with me? Don't you love me?" How unfair. How insecure. That neediness is only destroying their relationship, not helping it to grow stronger. Allow, no *encourage*, your partner to have interests and activities that have nothing to do with you.

The Freedom to Enjoy Togetherness.   The marriage vows imply we should hold to each other because we have to, not because we want to. I have learned that few people respond well to "have to." It's based in obligation. Obligation means we owe someone something. I don't want to owe someone. I don't want to spend time with someone out of obligation. I don't want to give love out of obligation. I know resentment stems from obligation and the feeling that you have to do something you may not really want to do. I certainly don't want to resent the person with whom I have chosen to spend my life. My wife and I are together because we want to be. We have been through too much to feel obligated. Obligation went out the door many years ago between us. We simply enjoy our time together. Nothing is sweeter than to turn down a "better offer" in order to just spend time with your partner simply because you know that's how you would rather spend your time.

Jealousy

My wife has many men friends—friends she has known for years, worked with for years, friends that I share, and many that I don't. She enjoys their friendship and has dinner with them when they are in town whether I am around or not. I'm not jealous one bit. She loves these men and they are true friends to her. However, they are not a threat to our marriage. The marriage is based on trust. I have the same arrangement. In fact, some of my closest friends are women. I don't have sexual feelings for them—yet I hug them when I see them and give them a smooch good-bye when we part. My wife isn't jealous, nor should she be. We both completely love these other people who are in our lives; however, we are in love only with each other.

Jealousy doesn't play a part in this love we have for other people. Jealousy is an emotion based in fear. It's a dangerous emotion that grows from a lack of self-esteem and a lack of trust. It's destructive in every way. It will destroy your relationships and your sanity. Give it up.

Trust

Once trust is broken, I'm not sure you can ever really get it back. At least not like it was before the trust was broken. My wife and I don't trust each other exactly the way we did before we messed up. We are not the same people we were before we messed up, so it's impossible to have the same relationship we used to have. The old trust we used to share doesn't work any longer, so we had to develop a new level of trust, which resulted in us having a whole new relationship. The only way to make any relationship that has been violated work again is to establish a new trust based on a new commitment.

The issue of trust applies to all relationships. Most people have a tendency to consider trust as a factor that exists only in marriages. But trust is a factor in all relationships: parent/child; boss/subordinate; friends/family members; company/customer; coworkers/corporations/stockholders. Each of these relationships relies on trust. Once it's broken, the relationship changes forever. And in each situation, the relationship pays a price.

Before you lie, steal, cheat, spread a rumor, talk behind someone's back, or disappoint someone needlessly, think about the consequences and know there is no going back. And if your relationship with another has been violated, don't think you can repair it. You can't. You can only start over by building a completely new relationship based on a new level of trust.

Communication

We have all been told the key to communication is to meet the other person halfway. Can't be done—doesn't work. What if you travel halfway and the other person only goes a fourth of the way?

That still leaves a gap, right? So how far should you go when it comes to establishing open communications? How about all the way? Sorry, but that's not far enough either. I have been in a conversation where I went all the way and my wife decided to turn around and go the other way. If you have ever tried having a conversation with your teenager, you know that you can go the entire way and they won't budge and will run either physically or emotionally to get away from you. So what is the right answer? As far as it takes. You go as far as it takes to establish open, honest communication. Not halfway, not all the way, but as far as it takes.

Just talk and keep talking, even though the communication may be painful. Silence isn't always your friend when trying to establish or maintain or heal a relationship. In conflict, silence is just easier than having a conversation and dealing with the problem, yet that route doesn't always bring about resolution. Because when silence becomes too comfortable, you end up becoming more and more distant. Most of the time you have to tough it out and just talk your way through things.

Disagreements

"Almost all married people fight, although many are ashamed to admit it. Actually, a marriage in which no quarreling takes place may well be one that is dead or dying from emotional undernourishment. If you care, you probably fight."
—Flora Davis

Any time two people are in a relationship there are going to be disagreements. At least I hope so. Can you imagine a relationship where there are no arguments? Can you imagine what kind of mealy-mouthed weaklings those people must be? I don't know who said it but I totally agree with the line, "When two people always agree, one of them is not necessary."

I have heard people say about some couple they know, "There was never a harsh word between them." What? My commentary on that relationship is, "Boring!" My wife and I fight. I scream and she replies in a calm, logical way which makes me scream all the louder. That's what passionate people do.

It's healthy and natural for people to argue. I actually enjoy it. (Bet that surprises you, doesn't it!) My wife hates it. I love expressing my opinions on just about anything to just about anyone who will listen. My wife doesn't enjoy the exchange of harsh words. She would rather keep her anger inside and bottle it up. That's the way her family did it and that's the way she learned to deal with disagreements. My family yelled and screamed and fought it all out. No one ever wondered how any other person in the family felt—we got it said. So for years, my wife would run from confrontation. She thought it meant we didn't love each other because we were in conflict with each other. It was a long process to convince her that just the opposite was true. So, she learned to argue with me. We proved we loved each other enough to express ourselves openly and honestly and get things dealt with and handled.

Don't let your anger stay bottled up until it turns into resentment. Don't let the sun go down on your issues. Express them. Deal with them. Get it said and then make up. (Sometimes making up can be so much fun you might want to consider starting an argument!)

The key to arguing is to make it about something and not about someone. Personal attacks are cheap shots and only hurt the relationship. A good healthy exchange about a topic doesn't hurt the relationship and can actually make it stronger. Steer clear of name-calling. Do your best not to attack the other person. Words said in anger can't be taken back, and those names you called him leave real wounds. Even when the other person did something you want to take issue with, keep the argument about what they did and not about who they are.

Reach Out and Touch

Babies who are not touched don't develop intellectually or emotionally as well as those who are cuddled and held. The same applies to adults. Any relationship where people don't touch will not flourish either.

When my wife and I were in counseling we were made to touch in some way while we argued, even if it was just to touch her foot with my toe. The touch created a bond between us even though all other bonds were nearly destroyed. The touch kept us connected in some small way.

Hug. Kiss. Pat. Hold hands. Whatever it takes to stay in physical contact. Why do you think people shake hands when they meet? It's to establish a physical bond that can then be built upon. Same thing when you make a deal with someone; you shake hands. What's the first thing two people are told to do when they are pronounced man and wife? They are told to kiss. It's the first physical bond of their new official life together, which can then be built upon.

The first thing that usually goes away when a couple has a problem is the physical contact. That's why our counselor wanted us to touch in some small way while we worked out our problems. When you touch there is an exchange of energy that will bring people closer.

Show physical affection to your partner in order to stay emotionally connected. And remember: Affection that comes from lack of obligation is the sweetest and most meaningful.

A How-To List for Being a Better Spouse

- Make a list of everything you like/love about your spouse. Be very specific. Then tell your spouse one of the things on the list every day.

- Make a list of everything you don't like about your spouse. Throw it away. You probably aren't going to be able to do much about it anyway, so move on.
- Make another list that describes the perfect spouse you would like to have. Become that list. Surprised you, didn't I? When you become the kind of spouse you would like to have, your chances of getting the spouse you want are more likely.
- Leave your spouse little notes saying how much you love him or her and why.
- Find ways to laugh together. Laughter is a powerful bond.
- Hug more. Gripe less.
- Scope up. Let pettiness go. So the top is off the toothpaste—let it slide.
- Treat your spouse with the same dignity and respect you would give to a stranger.
- Fulfill your spouse's fantasies from time to time. Do the unexpected. Keep the element of surprise alive.
- Have lots of sex. It's hard to be mad or stay mad at someone when you're doing them.

CHAPTER THIRTEEN

KIDS ARE A PAIN IN THE BUTT

Kids are dirty, messy, and expensive. They keep you from doing what you would like to do so you can drive them around to do what they want to do. They are selfish, demanding, grungy little creatures that destroy your house, your car, and about everything else you hold dear. There. It's been said. You know I'm right, and you probably always felt this way even about your own kids but you just couldn't admit it to yourself, could you?

However, they are the neatest things ever to happen to anyone. I love mine. I may not like yours and I certainly don't expect you to like mine, but I know you love yours just as I do mine.

Kids are just so cool. They are always on the lookout for a good time. They eat when they are hungry, sleep when they are tired, and love you even when you are being an idiot. (Yes, parents are sometimes idiots. Weren't yours?) And they are your responsibility. You are responsible for what they learn and how they act. Kids act the way they do because they were taught to act that way.

IT ISN'T THE KIDS' FAULT

You know those little kids you see in the mall and in restaurants that are just so bad? The ones who throw their food, run all over the place screaming, and make everyone around them miserable? The ones so ill-behaved you just want to jerk them up yourself and take control of the situation? Those kids drive me crazy! What I have to remind myself is that the little kids are not bad at all and don't need to be spanked or scolded. There are no bad little kids; there are only bad parents. It isn't the kid's fault he is running around the restaurant screaming like a banshee; it's the parents' fault. The little kid doesn't need to be reprimanded, the mama and daddy do. Little kids behave exactly the way they are allowed to behave—no better, no worse. They push their limits. They are supposed to push their limits; it's part of growing up. It's the responsibility of parents to set limits and boundaries for the child to live within, then discipline accordingly when they don't.

DISCIPLINE IS A MUST

Parents, you must love your kids enough to discipline them. A lack of discipline is simply a lack of love. I am not saying you should spank them or stand them in a corner or give them a time out. That is your business and there are people much more qualified than I to talk about those things. Just be consistent in your discipline and try to make the punishment fit the crime. And please, please, please do it privately. Don't scream and smack your kid in front of the rest of us. It's embarrassing to the kid and to all who have to witness it.

When I was growing up, my dad would often say, "When we get home you are going to get a whipping." My dad gave hard whippings with a belt. Not abusive and not all that often, but when I got one, I did not soon forget it. It did not matter whether he told me that on the first day of a two-week vacation—when we got home, even though not one more word had been said about it for the entire two weeks, I still got my whipping. My dad taught me a lot with those whippings. The lesson was not just about what I got the whipping for—that was obvious. The real lesson was that his word was golden. A promise is a promise regardless of what the promise is about. Though I did not appreciate that lesson much when I was promised a whipping, I appreciate it now. I learned I could count on what he told me, every time, good or bad. I have tried to teach the same lesson to my children.

THE IMPORTANCE OF YOUR WORD

My boys and I play a game based on the idea "What would you do for how much money?" Stupid stuff like how much money would it take to eat a worm? Or bite the head off a chicken? Just silly stuff we were willing to put a price on and laugh about. (By the way, my price was always much lower than theirs. I know what it takes to make the big bucks and somehow a worm or a chicken head doesn't seem like that big a deal to me.)

When my boys were about five and nine years old, we were out taking our dogs, Elvis and Nixon, for a walk. I had some dog biscuits in my pocket and I asked my older son, Tyler, what it would take for him to eat a dog biscuit. He said he would eat one if I ate one. I immediately popped one in my mouth, chewed it up, and swallowed it with a smile and then handed him his. He wouldn't do it. He said he was just kidding.

That is when he learned a very valuable life-lesson: A deal is a deal. I wouldn't let him off the hook. I made it very clear he would eat the dog biscuit just like I did. He made the rules and he was going to live by them. We stood right there in the street for a good long while with him whining about how he did not really mean it. That is when he learned the next valuable life-lesson: Don't let your mouth write a check your ass can't cash. I told him we would stand right there all night if we had to, but in the end, he would indeed eat the dog biscuit.

Finally, reluctantly, he ate it. Some would say after reading that story that I am a harsh father. I disagree. I think it was a moment that influenced his life forever. Now that he is a man, we laugh about that story and he brags about how his dad taught him a lot when I made him eat a dog biscuit.

Few people ever really learn that a deal is a deal and they write a check nearly every day that their ass can't cash. I think they should have to eat a dog biscuit.

What have you taught your children? Have you taught them that television is more important than talking? Have you taught them that cheating on your taxes is perfectly all right because, after all, it's the government and not a real person who is being taken advantage of? What do they learn from you when they see you belittle your employees or talk behind your friend's back? Or how you talk to your own father or mother? What lesson is being taught with those words?

Your kids are a reflection of what you have taught them. And just like you have always heard, your actions speak louder than your words.

I have tried to teach my children some good lessons. I have taught my children what a good hamburger is and what great barbeque is all about. I have taught them that Elvis is The King. In my opinion, those are important lessons! The rest I watched them pick up from being around me. My older son, Tyler, knows how to take responsibility. When he messes up, he freely admits it and moves toward a solution to fix the problem. My younger son, Patrick, has discovered his uniqueness. He isn't afraid to be different and is completely confident in his individuality. Neither will lie—not to me or to anyone else. They say what they feel and let the chips fall where they may. They can be counted on. Always.

Raising kids isn't easy. In fact, it's the hardest thing I know of. It's the most awesome responsibility ever assigned a human being. And while I certainly don't know all there is to know about being a great parent, I have figured out a handful of good ideas.

THEY GROW OUT OF IT

This is my number-one piece of parenting advice. Every time I got overly concerned about something going on in one of my kids' lives, I wish someone had been there with this piece of advice. My son, Patrick, went through a stage when he got his body pierced: ears, nose, lip, navel, eyebrow, nipples—if you can think of a place on his upper body, it had a hole with jewelry in it. I hated it, but I kept my mouth shut. After all, I had my ears pierced and did not have too much room to complain. In just a matter of months every piercing had disappeared. He got bored with it. That happens with kids. Things come and go. The key sometimes is to keep your mouth shut about it and let it slide. If it's something serious, like guns and drugs or something life threatening, then you should get very involved. But a piercing is just not that serious. Pick your battles but don't make everything a battle. Holes grow back. Purple hair grows out. Baggy butt clothes go out of style. Hats eventually turn around so the bill is in the front. Kids do become human again.

Besides, as you already know, the more hell you raise about something, the more dead set they are to do it. I think kids wait for you to hate something just so they can decide they like it. It's a game they play with their parents. It's fun for them. Be careful when you play the game because they usually win at this one.

STAY INVOLVED

Know what is going on in your kids' lives. Know what their interests are. Know their friends. Have their friends over to your house for a party. Yes, they will trash your house, but it's better to have a messed-up house than it is a dead kid. Yes, I said dead kid. Kids die these days. There are guns and drugs and suicide and pedophiles to deal with. We did not have as many of those things to deal with when we were younger. Kids today deal with much more serious stuff than we ever did. One of the best ways to fight this is by keeping your kids involved and by being involved with them. Know who they hang around with, know where they go, and have their friends come to your house so you can be close—not to meddle in their business, but just so you will be there if needed.

GIVE THEM THEIR PRIVACY, BUT KNOW WHAT IS GOING ON

Don't read their e-mail or their diaries. Don't be a snoop. You need to stay informed, but if you violate their privacy they will resent you and cut you off from any and all information. If you really want to know what is going on, then establish a relationship based on open communication, trust, and respect. Then you won't have to resort to being a snoop in order to stay informed.

BE COOL, BUT NOT TOO COOL

Be the kind of parent your kids can talk to. But don't be their best friend. Don't try to be one of the gang. My boys and I are friends but I am still their dad. We can openly talk about anything in the world—and I mean anything. Yet, there is a line between being their best friend and still being their father that we don't cross.

I always think it's sad when I see mothers and fathers trying to be their kid's best friend. Kids should pick their own friends.

Let them. Don't be such a needy parent that you require your children to pick you as their best friend.

BE REALISTIC—KIDS MESS UP

Don't expect perfection. Kids are not perfect. They are kids. Especially when it comes to grades. Good grades are not worth crying over. Good grades are not worth sacrificing social balance over. Ask your kids to do their best, help them do their best, then teach them to be satisfied with their results.

The short list for raising good kids:

- If you have little bitty kids, sit on the floor a lot. Communicate at their level.
- Teach them about money. How to earn it, save it, invest it, spend it, and give it away.
- Listen to them.
- Ask more, tell less.
- Hug more, nag less.
- Show your kids affection even after they think they are too big for it.
- Teach them the really important things: kindness, charity, love, forgiveness, compassion, respect, honesty, responsibility, and how to have fun.
- Never lie to them. Never tolerate any lie from them.
- Encourage your children to develop their own uniqueness. Don't try to mold their personalities. Let them be who they are and let them become what they want to become, not what you want them to become.
- Don't make a jackass out of yourself at their sporting events.

- Don't protect them too much. Let them make their own mistakes and suffer the consequences. The lesson is in the consequences.
- They need love more than stuff.

TEENAGERS

Teenagers are such an anomaly that they get their own section. They are obnoxious, rude, self-absorbed, pretty much disgusting creatures. There is no known cure, except time. While they do eventually grow out of it, it's always just in the nick of time.

Whey my older son was 16, he went toe-to toe with me, telling me he no longer had to do what I said because he was bigger than I was. He was right—he was bigger. But I quickly reminded him I was smarter, I had all the money, and I knew where he slept. I told him I did not see any cure for our relationship except euthanasia; we were just going to have to put him to sleep. I loved him. I just could not stand him.

Have you been there with your kids? If not, chances are you will be. Few kids are immune to being a teenager.

My only advice for you regarding teenagers is to do whatever it takes to keep from killing them for a couple of years. Mine actually made it through the tough times in about six months. He is lucky; he was so close!

Too much testosterone or estrogen in too short a period of time makes a kid stupid. You went through the same stuff and you grew out of it. At least I hope you did.

Just bite your tongue. Leave the room. Shut their bedroom door so you don't have to look at their mess. Do whatever it takes. Just keep loving them no matter what they say or do and almost always it will work out okay. Eventually.

There are many signs that parents aren't doing a good job as parents. All you have to do is look around at the millions of people living out the results of their own bad parenting to know that. Take a moment and look at these ten signs and evaluate how you are doing:

Ten signs you are a bad parent:

1. If you don't know where your child is right now, you are a bad parent.
2. If your child is obese, you are a bad parent.
3. If your child has a television in their bedroom, you are a bad parent.
4. If you don't know your child's friends, you are a bad parent.
5. If you tolerate disrespect from your child verbally or physically, you are a bad parent.
6. If you promise consequences for either good behavior or bad behavior and don't deliver, you are a bad parent.
7. If you don't teach your child about money, you are a bad parent.
8. If you don't have open, honest communication with your child about sex—the dangers, consequences, and joy of it—you are a bad parent.
9. If your grown child still lives at home and mooches off you, you are a bad parent.
10. If your own life is an example of what you don't want your child to grow up and become, you are a bad parent.

Some of you are now spewing and sputtering and shouting "yeah but" at me because your kids are great, yet they have a TV in their room or are overweight or blah, blah, blah-de-blah-de-blah! Okay, you can tell yourself that, and since I don't know you or your kid I'll step back and give you the benefit of the doubt. But just because you don't see the harmful results of your action or lack of action today, doesn't mean that you won't later.

"But I genuinely *love* my kids, Larry!" I'm sure you do. But we have to stop pretending that the definition of being a good parent is "loving your child." Parenting is more than love. Parenting is loving your child enough to make sure you produce a responsible, productive, fit adult who lives a life steeped in honesty, integrity, and respect. An adult with a strong work ethic who knows how to give her word and keep it even when it isn't convenient. A person who knows how to be financially responsible by earning, investing, saving, giving, and enjoying their money. That requires communication, involvement, education, discipline, and punishment. It requires work. Love without the actions to back it up doesn't really mean much.

If you want more information about parenting the Larry way, read my bestselling book, *Your Kids Are Your Own Fault: A Guide for Raising Responsible, Productive Adults.*

CHAPTER FOURTEEN

SEX: GOTTA LOVE IT

"We're all so busy acquiring things, when all we really want to do is get naked."

—Jason Purcell

Sex is the coolest thing on the planet and our society has done its best to make it wrong and dirty. We try to legislate it. That doesn't work. We try to limit it. That doesn't work either. We try to make it appear nasty so people won't want to do it so much. That doesn't work for sure. In fact, that only makes us want to do it more. So why does none of this work? It's not supposed to. Sex is to be enjoyed. It's natural. Anything done to inhibit sexual expression will always backfire, because it's a natural thing.

Sexual repression is the cause of many crimes—not sexual expression. Sexual repression is the cause of much guilt—not sexual expression. Sexual repression finances the lives of many psychologists, therapists, and writers—not sexual expression. Sexual repression ruins more relationships and marriages than almost any other factor I know of—not sexual expression.

I know you can come up with some exceptions here and so can I. There are always exceptions, but you must admit I make a very good point.

Think about it. Did you ever hear anyone complain because they were getting too much sex? I don't think so.

Remember the 1960s? I know, I know, some of you don't, but maybe you saw the mini-series or bought the soundtrack. In the 1960s, protesters carried a sign that said, "Make Love, Not War." Know what? They were right.

It's impossible to shoot another person or kill another person while you are having sex. Well, not impossible, but highly unlikely.

So am I saying just go have irresponsible sex with whomever you can? Absolutely not. I say be responsible.

"Sex can bring magic into a relationship, and anchor it in a way that no amount of talking or doing things together can."
　　　　　　　　　　　　　　—Thomas Moore, *Soul Mates*

Sex isn't wrong. Sex is very right. That is the message we should be teaching our children. That is the message we should be telling ourselves every day of our lives. We need to give ourselves permission to enjoy it—in all of its forms.

"Wait! In all of its forms?"

Yes.

"Oh no! You aren't saying. . . ."

Yes.

"But that's wrong."

Who says so?

"God did."

Did She?

"Yes, He did."

Then leave it to God to judge, even though She won't. You stay out of it. Really. Just do the world a favor and butt out. It's none of your business.

SEX WITH YOUR CHOSEN PARTNER

Make it exciting. Use toys. Have phone sex. Send each other erotic e-mails. Get some whipped cream and massage oil. Candles and bubble bath are always good. Get creative. Get a good fantasy life going. Talk dirty to each other. Just about anything goes as long as both consent. If it feels good, do it. If you both agree to it, do it. Just enjoy each other.

"But I don't have anyone else to enjoy."

Well, enjoy yourself then.

"?"

You understand.

And remember this about sex: If you are not sweating, you are doing something wrong.

"Is sex dirty? Only if it's done right."

—Woody Allen

Kids and Sex

Abstinence doesn't work. Don't expect it to. I doubt it worked with you when you were a kid, so don't expect it to work with your kids either. It won't. They are going to do it. You probably did. (If not, then it's no wonder you are such a mess!)

We should teach our kids there is nothing wrong with doing it. It's natural, normal, and as far as I can tell the most fun you are ever going to have—without exception. However, there are guidelines that provide a foundation on which to build every sexual relationship. These are the guidelines that we much teach our kids:

Respect

Responsibility

Safety

These are the three things we should teach our kids about sex. They will figure out what goes where all on their own, but few parents will teach them these three things. Parents and other adults should stop telling kids that sex is bad. It isn't. We should stop telling them they are going to ruin their lives by doing it. They are not. Most of all, we should stop telling them they are going to go to hell if they do it. They won't.

My sons lived with their mother growing up, and they attended a large Protestant church that asked them to sign agreements saying they would never engage in sex prior to marriage. Actually, this is a common practice in many religious organizations and fundamentalist denominations. And it's nothing but guilt producing. It teaches kids that sex is wrong. And it isn't.

All of this guilt-producing teaching hasn't done one thing to cut back on sexual activity among young adults. It hasn't cut back on sexual crimes or teenage pregnancy. The only thing I can see it has done is create a society of sexually repressed people who don't understand how to have sex without guilt. Do you find that sad?

So am I condoning premarital sex? Yes. If more couples did it before they got married there would be fewer unhappy marriages and fewer divorces.

Am I saying that kids should have sex? No. I am saying that kids are going to have sex. Teach them how to do it responsibly. Teach them that no means no—every time and without exception. Educate them about sexually transmitted diseases and about birth control. We ask kids to be responsible and yet we as parents are totally irresponsible when we don't teach our kids how to handle something as powerful as sex.

CHAPTER FIFTEEN

CRITICISM HAPPENS

There are two kinds of criticism: the kind you give and the kind you get.

Let me first deal with your criticism of others. It's so easy to do, right? And some of it is just natural. You don't like the way people act and it bugs you to the point that you say something about it. No big deal, in my opinion. In fact, it's how I make my living pretty much. I see stupidity and I criticize it. That kind of criticism is a normal thing. Then there is the kind of criticism where you say something silly like, "I can't believe she is wearing that!" Again, a natural thing to do and no biggy. Criticism becomes dangerous when it's directed at who someone is, and not what they do. No one really has the right to talk about who another person is.

"But isn't that what you are doing in this book, Larry?"

Not at all. In this book I am attacking the actions people take and their results. I am criticizing a lack of personal responsibility. I am criticizing bad thinking that doesn't produce good results. Because I am blunt about it, it confuses some folks because they consider any criticism to be rude, condescending, and personal. I can assure you that isn't the case.

Not long ago, I watched a segment of *60 Minutes* with Supreme Court Justice Antonin Scalia. Justice Scalia was talking about Justice Ruth Bader Ginsberg and how they have such an unlikely friendship. After all, you have Scalia, a true conservative, and Ginsberg, a liberal. He said, "I attack ideas, not people, and there are very good people with very bad ideas." I like that. I hope I do the same. I never want to attack another human being on a personal level. I do, however, feel I have the right to attack the behavior of individuals. So do you. In fact, I encourage you to do so.

As an employer, you certainly have the right to criticize your employee's behavior. You have the right to both monitor and enforce your position about that employee's behavior. If you don't like the behavior, you can attack it and correct it and work on that behavior until you get it the way you want it to be; after all, you are paying for it. If you can't fix the behavior, I think the employee should be fired so they can go someplace where their behavior fits the job better than it did for you. But I want to make sure that it's about the behavior. It's not about the employee. If you don't like the person, that isn't part of the deal; you aren't paying for their personality. You are paying for that person's results . . . period. Manage and judge the worth of an employee based on their results, not their personality.

The same applies to your children. When your kid messes up (and they will), you don't attack the kid. You simply attack the kid's behavior. The same applies to everyone else in your family and your friends. In fact, being a true friend is the ability to give (and receive) honest feedback on stupid behavior. A true friend will grab you by the shoulders, look you in the eye, and say "You are being an idiot! Stop it." When a friend does that to you—thank them!

Good people do stupid, idiotic things. Criticize the action, the behavior, and the result, but not the person.

WHEN OTHERS CRITICIZE YOU

Some criticism is personal, however. It's meant to hurt you. I know you have experienced it just as I have.

When you create the life you have always wanted, you will be criticized. It won't be fair; in fact it might not even be rational. That probably means you are on the right track.

"Great spirits have always encountered violent opposition from mediocre minds."

—Albert Einstein

People who create the life they have dreamed should consider themselves to be great spirits. They have set themselves apart from most of society (the mediocre minds) and made something great happen. And this will really bother those who have chosen mediocrity.

Mediocre people will be intimidated by your success. That's because they haven't been willing to do what it takes to achieve their dreams, so their retaliation is to attack you for doing what they haven't been willing to do. A lot of them are convinced that, because you are successful, you have used up some of the success that is available for them. You have stolen some of what they could have had if they had only gone after it. They have no idea there is plenty available for all who choose to participate. They are convinced there is a limited supply and you have taken more than your share and robbed them of their share.

It's not that they don't want you to be successful. It's just that they don't want you to be more successful than they are. The people who say they are your "friends" and criticize your success are mostly afraid that you will move on and leave them behind. After all, you aren't going to have the time to waste trashing other people, or to take extended breaks and lunch hours, or to gripe and whine about the high cost of living and how mean and cruel the world is. Actually, that is a valid fear and will probably happen. Once you become successful you will choose differently.

You won't have time for things that move you away from your goal. That includes people who hold you back.

However, the biggest fear people have is fear of themselves. They are afraid that they don't have the ability or the guts to do what you have done. They are scared to death to go to the mirror and take responsibility for their lives or to take the action they know is necessary to turn their situation around. And they channel this self-fear and doubt into criticism of you.

They will criticize you to your face and behind your back. They will make little jokes about how you are moving up. They will try to get others to side with them, and sadly some will do it. You can't do much about it, so don't bother trying. You can't change these people. You can't bring them with you on the road to success. All people must follow their own path when they are ready to make the journey.

Don't bother defending your success. You have nothing to defend. You took advantage of your talents and abilities. You went to work on yourself and your life and now you are reaping the benefits. You did well as a result of serving others well. You have been rewarded for the work you put in. You sacrificed and you put in the hours and paid the price, so enjoy it. You deserve everything you have. You did it. Just you. Don't apologize for it. Don't be embarrassed by it. Simply be grateful and enjoy it. You can only achieve true happiness when you rise above the approval of others.

A guaranteed way to avoid criticism:

"Say nothing. Do nothing. Be nothing."

—Unknown

However, the ability to handle criticism is tough for some. They can't deal with the cruelty and stupidity of other people.

Many times it's because of a sense of entitlement that they are special and that no one has the right to tell them otherwise—blame Mama and Daddy for that one! These people need to grow up and realize they aren't special and that part of life is dealing with the criticism of others.

Others just rely too heavily on the opinions of others. They base their self-acceptance on whether others accept them. That's a sad way to live. In essence, you are handing over your happiness to someone else when you must have the approval of other people. You must learn to be strong and deal with the criticism of others. Criticism happens in life and in the workplace, and people who can't handle criticism are doomed to be victims and people who dish it out unfairly are called bullies. However, let me give you a different twist on the whole issue of bullying.

You Can't Have a Bully without a Victim. Bullying is all over the news these days. And it's a damn shame. It's a shame that it happens and it's a shame that people who get bullied feel that the way to cope with it is to commit an act of deadly violence against themselves. But the problem isn't always the bully. Bullies will always exist as long as there are people who are willing to be bullied. Bullying isn't so much about the bully as it is about being a victim. You can't bully someone who refuses to be a victim.

The bullying issue stems from believing that the opinions of other people actually matter. Society is obsessed with the opinions of other people. We believe that things like wearing a certain brand, carrying a certain cell phone, watching a certain television show will help us gain the approval of other people. And sadly, it will. We base our entire lives on whether others like us instead of whether we like ourselves. We have become much more interested in others approving of who we are rather than approving of ourselves. We see people on television regularly sell their souls seemingly just to become popular or famous. It seems that we have thrown self-esteem (the act of holding one's self in high esteem) out the window in order to have other's-esteem (the act of wanting others to hold us in high esteem). Yeah, I made that one up, but I like it: *other's-esteem*. And it's that other's-esteem that is causing the problem. All of us need to be reminded of the title of that great book by Terry Cole-Whittaker, *What You Think of Me Is None of My Business*. When we learn to think in those terms we can rise above the approval of others and not be controlled and manipulated by the words and actions of others.

That's why and how bullying really occurs in the first place: putting the approval of others above the approval of one's self. Sadly, making the opinion of other people so important that when we don't receive it, some are willing to commit suicide because of it. I know many of you are going to say that the cases I am citing were more extreme than simply not receiving the approval of others. You are right. But there is a starting point for all of this and it starts with wanting others to approve of us, and then not being able to accept it when we don't get it. It also starts with self-approval and self-acceptance. I contend that when we teach our children not to care what others think but instead to become people who love, accept, and honor themselves, much of the bullying will disappear. Let me be clear on this one: Bullies won't disappear, but bullying will, simply because there won't be any victims for them to prey upon.

We need to learn that 100 percent peer approval is an unrealistic goal. We need to understand that there will always be people who will demean you, not because you deserve it but simply because they have their own problems they haven't come to deal with yet, and the only way they know to build themselves up is to put others down. In other words, some people simply don't like themselves and feel good only when they are making fun of others. And some people are just jerks. These jerks will always exist. You can't legislate against them nor can you sue them for being rude and unkind. But we all need to understand that you can't hold *them* accountable for *your* reaction to their unkindness.

It's much like blaming a bartender for the fact you drank too much and ended up drunk and then did something horrible in your condition. Your actions are your choices. You are the one in control. You don't have to let someone influence your actions. You don't have to be victimized by anyone else. It's about choice and personal responsibility.

If you tease me and call me names and embarrass me and I go out and kill someone, I am the one who is going to be held responsible for the murder. Seems to me that the same applies when it comes to suicide. If you tease me and call me names and embarrass me and I kill myself, it's *my* fault, not yours. You simply can't blame the bully for the personal actions of the one who is bullied. I know this isn't a popular opinion. But suicide isn't the result of bullying. People who commit suicide feel that is their only option. They feel there is no other solution. Therefore they implement a permanent solution to a temporary problem. And if there was ever a temporary problem, it's being bullied. Bullies come and go. You have a bully for a while, but then they move on to another victim. Then you move along and another bully shows up. But the issue is the personal responsibility of how you react to the bully. Do you give up control to the bully? Do you allow someone else to dictate your reaction? No. You stop being a victim so the bully has to go elsewhere to find someone to bully.

In stating this case to others, some have said that my approach is calloused and I would feel differently if it were my son or daughter. I hope I wouldn't. I would surely be devastated, but I hope I would realize that my job as a parent was to teach my child to be a strong individual who was able to stand up to the criticism and actions of others, even when that criticism and those actions were extremely hurtful. And if the worst happened I would be sorry that I didn't teach my child to rise above the approval of others. I would be sorry that I didn't help my child learn how to love themselves enough that what others say and do just doesn't matter in the long run. I would be sorry that I didn't teach my child that there are options available to deal with these issues and that suicide is never one of them.

And within those statements lies the solution: Parenting. I spoke a lot about bullying in my bestseller, *Your Kids Are Your Own Fault*. If you don't have the book, get it and read it. It's up to parents to teach their children not be victims. It's up to parents to teach their kids how to hold themselves in high esteem and to think well of themselves. It's up to parents to teach their kids how to handle criticism because the sad fact is, people are always going to criticize you. And yes, it's up to parents to teach their kids not to pick on others, not to bully others, and to be nice to others. Bullies are the result of bad parenting. But so are victims.

I taught my kids that if they were bullied it's the other kid's problem, not theirs. I taught them to think that the other kid was an idiot for being mean to them and to write that kid off as a jerk and to move on. I taught them to live the old saying, "Sticks and stones may break my bones but words will never hurt me." While we all know that saying is a lie and that words do hurt, it's still important to teach kids that hurtful words come from people who are weak and to be pitied and are not to be considered truthful words to be taken seriously from a reliable source. It's also important to teach kids that they are only words.

I also taught my kids that it was acceptable to physically defend themselves against getting punched in the nose and physically abused by bullies. My dad taught me that it was better to nurse a bloody nose than to lose your dignity. I agree. Hit back when someone hits you. Some say that is promoting violence. Really? I don't believe that violence is the first answer to any problem, but I'll be damned if I let my kid's face be used as a punching bag by letting his arms dangle at his sides while he tries to reason with an obnoxious kid. My kid may get in trouble for fighting at school and I may take criticism as a parent, but I'll deal with the aftermath of my kid hitting back in order to save his nose and his dignity.

I also think it's important for parents to take a good look at their own kid when she is playing victim to a bully. Is she being ridiculed, made fun of, and called names for being fat? Is she fat? If she is, then help her lose weight. As the parent, her being overweight is your fault and you are aiding and abetting the bully by allowing her to be that way. Don't blame another kid for calling it as it's just because they hurt your child's feelings doing so.

Is your kid annoying? Yes, your little darling might be annoying, so recognize it and deal with your kid's annoying ways so others won't pick on him.

Does your kid look like a victim? Don't pretend you don't know what I mean. The world is full of people who *look* like victims, and you see them every day just as I do. Some people just look like they are ready to get their butt kicked. They don't carry themselves with confidence, walk with confidence, or speak with confidence. If that is your kid, teach them to stand up straight, look people in the eye, speak up, and look like they are in control of their physical space. That way people won't even consider violating their space. It's your job as a parent to do so. "They are just shy" isn't an excuse that is going to help them be successful as an adult, so teach them to move past it as a child.

Is your kid gay? Are they scared to death to tell you because they know you won't approve of them and that your love is conditional on them being straight? How do you expect them to approve of themselves and feel okay about who they really are when you don't? If you don't love them for who they are, they aren't going to love themselves either. Your job is to teach your child how to develop a healthy self-esteem so they will carry themselves with confidence, feel good about themselves, and love the person they really are.

Teaching your child to disregard the negative comments of others is a challenge. Children can be mean. And mean children can grow into mean adults. I run into rude, mean, negative, hurtful people every day, don't you? These people are your boss, your co-workers, siblings, friends, and maybe even your spouse. Everyone knows a bully and may have even been a bully from time to time. If we all crumbled every time someone said something mean to us, we couldn't survive in the workplace. If we fell to pieces every time someone cut us off in traffic we would have to park our car and stay home. Life is full of bullies. I rarely go a day without a run-in with one. I can't do a thing about it except refuse to be their victim. That's a lesson we all need to learn. That's a lesson you *must* teach your child.

But Bullies Aren't Just for Kids, Bullies Are in the Workplace Too. Bullies in the workplace come in all shapes and sizes. Sometimes it's the boss, sometimes a co-worker, and sometimes it's the guy in charge of supplies who won't give you any staples or the little old receptionist who won't put your calls through. Sometimes, the bully is even your customer. What do you do?

Bullies in the workplace are the same as bullies in the schoolyard. They are primarily cowards and don't know what to do when you stand up to them. So stand up to them. Again, remember my rule for bullies: You can only have a bully if you have a victim. If you refuse to be a victim to the bully, they will move on. If you are forced to deal with a bully in the workplace, check this list:

1. Ask yourself why you are being bullied. Do you appear weak? Are you weak? Are you doing something to provoke this person? Look at yourself first.
2. Confront the bully. Look them in the eye and ask why? Then speak up and tell them that you refuse to accept it any longer and clearly communicate exactly what you *do* expect in the future. Remember: Communicate expectations and communicate what you intend to do if the expectations are not met.

3. Keep your word by doing what you said you would do. If you threatened to report them, then report them.

4. Don't show weakness, don't apologize, don't lose your temper, and remember this in the workplace: Document everything. Bullies run on emotion; fight them with documentation.

CHAPTER SIXTEEN

SOMETIMES WORK IS JUST PLAIN WORK

Try as you might, there's just no way around it. At some point, you have to work. Work is a part of everyone's life. I haven't figured out a way to avoid it, though it seems to me that some have perfected it to an art form. Those aren't people you want to emulate, however. Work is a given, not just because it's the major source of your income but also because it's the major source of both your personal and professional fulfillment and satisfaction.

However, to those who say, "Just love what you do and you will never work a day in your life"—I say bull! Those people are idiots. No matter how much you love what you do, sometimes it's work! And sometimes it won't be fun. And sometimes you will hate it. Even if what you do is the true fulfillment of all the creative energy you have in your heart, mind, body, and soul, sometimes you will get tired of it and hate it. That is reality.

Here is the reality of work. You only really do what you do a small percentage of the time. In fact, if you look at just about any profession, you wind up actually doing the profession about 10 percent of the time, and the other 90 percent of the time you do the things that support the 10 percent.

For instance, in a sales job you only spend about 10 percent of your time actually selling. The other 90 percent is spent traveling to or from appointments, making phone calls, placing orders, going to meetings, talking to other departments, filling out paperwork, and many other things that have little to do with actual selling. Can you get out of it? I doubt it. It comes with the territory. Do you like it? Maybe, maybe not. It doesn't really matter whether you like it—it's just part of the deal.

It really doesn't matter much what you do for a living; you will find that very little time is spent doing it. Are you a plumber? How much time do you actually spend with tools in your hand? My guess is about 10 percent. Are you a piano tuner? How much time do you spend in front of a piano? About 10 percent. Are you a manager? How much of your time is actually spent managing? About 10 percent. A fitness trainer? How much time do you spend with a client actually training? Again, I'm betting about 10 percent.

I hate what I do for a living. Wait! You probably think this is what I do for a living? Nope, in the big scheme of things, I spend very little time writing books. Speaking? I spend about 75 hours per year on stage speaking. I love the time I spend being creative and putting my thoughts on paper, but the time spent messing with the book after that, I hate. I love my 75 hours on stage, but the 200 days a year I travel to make it happen, I hate. In other words, I love what I do about 10 percent of the time and hate what I do the other 90 percent of the time. The key to all of this is that we all have to love the 10 percent enough to put up with the 90 percent.

The good news is that none of us are paid to love our jobs. You aren't. You never got a check notated in the notes section, "Because he loves his job." You got your check because you did your job, not because you loved your job. If you love your job, that is a bonus.

WORK ISN'T ENOUGH

Don't automatically think that working hard will make you successful. It won't. I know lots of people who work very hard, much harder than I do, and don't really find any financial success. On the other hand, I don't know of anyone who has experienced real financial success who hasn't worked hard to achieve it. And don't offer me lottery winners or people who have inherited their money—they don't count. I'm talking about regular people like you and me. For us, it takes work.

"But Larry, I go to work every day and work hard!" I doubt it. Most studies say that workers waste at least two hours a day goofing off. Most admit to doing less than their best on the job and less than their best for the customer. So stop trying to fool yourself into believing that you are the hardest worker that was ever employed by anyone. It's probably just not true. You may be a hard worker and if you are, I applaud you for it. But the reality is that most people do just enough to keep from getting fired. Most people don't give their best effort. Most people don't do everything they were hired to do or are paid to do. That's reality, like it or not.

As a result, most people end up settling for much less than they have to mainly because they are just too lazy to work for what they really want. They do a half-assed job when they are on the job and then put little effort into living their dream when they go home. Life, happiness, prosperity, and success all take effort. If it feels easy, you are going the wrong direction. So don't think you can find true success without work, but don't think that work alone will give you success.

WHY BUSINESSES EXIST

They exist to make money. If you don't understand that, you are naïve. If you think they exist to make you happy or to take care of you, then you are going to be extremely disappointed. They are all about making money. Get this straight from the start and you will be much better off. The more you contribute to their making money, the more necessary you will become. The less you contribute to their profitability, the more expendable you become. See how simple it is? Your purpose is to help your company make money. It's no more complicated than that.

How can you help your company make money? That's not so hard either.

Three reasons you go to work every single day:

1. To keep existing customers.
2. To create new customers.
3. To make yourself and your organization the kind that other people want to do business with.

That is it. Those are the reasons you go to work every single day. Of course, I know many of you will immediately reject these reasons by saying you don't have customers, but you do. Everyone has customers. You might call them something else, but you still have customers. You might call them clients. In the medical community, you would call them patients. In education, students. In my world, the audience. You might also call them co-workers or employees. The thing to remember is this: Your job requires you to serve others. Even if you are the boss, you must serve your employees. As Bob Dylan sang, "You gotta serve somebody." Bob was right. All of us have to serve somebody. And in business, I call that "somebody" the customer.

To Keep Existing Customers

The lifeblood of any organization is its existing customer base. These are the people who are already doing business with you—the people who know you, trust you, and have paid you for your services. Keeping them is your primary reason for going to work each day. You want repeat business. You need repeat business. You want these people to know you, love you, and to tell their friends about you. And these good people who have done business with you and who keep coming back to you are the people who will forgive you when you make a mistake, because you will make a mistake. We all do. They will forgive you because they know you can do better and have done better in the past. When shown some appreciation, these customers and their loyalty can help you survive the toughest of times and help you prosper during the best of times. They are your best friends. Treat them right!

To Create New Customers

Some people think this should actually be the number-one reason for going to work. Many have argued this point with me but I can assure you they are wrong. Creating new customers can't be first; it must be second. Did you ever see a company that neglected existing customers in order to pursue new customers? When that happens, those existing customers will go someplace else and become new customers for a new company. How sad. Those customers belonged to a company that blew it by either ignoring them or by treating them poorly. So the customers went elsewhere.

That is probably how you got your new customers—someone else didn't treat them right. Now it's your turn to get new customers and all you really have to do is treat them right. You don't have to be cheaper and sometimes you don't even have to be better than your competition. You just have to treat people better.

Then once those customers have done business with you, they become your existing customers and it's your chance to treat them well so they won't go elsewhere again.

To Make Yourself and Your Organization the Kind That Other People Want to Do Business With

This is actually the toughest reason of all. The other reasons are primarily based on your activities. This one is based on the kind of person you are. And when you add together the combined personalities and values of all who work at your business, you come up with an organization that has a personality and a set of values. The values and personality of any organization are only a reflection of the values and personality of its individual employees' personalities. Got it? And it doesn't matter what the plaques on the walls say. I have gone into many businesses that put big banners and plaques on the wall proclaiming how they feel about their customers. This stuff is proudly displayed so all customers will know exactly how the company feels about them. The problem is that they forgot to tell the employees. Yet, customers don't do business with companies, they do business with the employees of the company. That is where the belief in customers must start—with the people who have direct contact with the customers.

Ever had to get your driver's license renewed? Or get a new license plate for your car? I will bet the minute you walked into the Department of Motor Vehicles you got an overwhelming feeling that said, "This isn't going to be a pleasant experience." The very air in the room screamed that at you. All businesses scream at you. It usually isn't as noticeable as it is when you enter a government-run organization, but it exists.

Evaluate your company. What feeling do your customers get about you and your organization when they do business with you? Do your customers get the feeling you really care about their satisfaction? Or do they get the feeling they are just one more bozo that has to be put up with?

Some Short Lessons about Work

When you work, work! When you play, play! Don't mix the two. It only screws up the work *and* the play. This is especially true if you work at home. Be able to walk away. I have a home office. Many people have home offices these days. Sadly, many people are not good at having a home office. They just don't get much work done. Or even more sadly, they don't get much living done. You must be able to walk away from "home" and its duties and responsibilities to go to "work" and take on those duties and responsibilities. More important, you have to be able to walk away from the work and live your life. It's hard for some people. This requires great discipline but is necessary to your quality of life and quality of work!

Make your work area a place where you only do work things. Don't eat at your desk or do any personal things at your desk. When you aren't working, stay away from that area. If your work area has a door, then close it. If it doesn't have a door, put one in! Close off the area where you work from the place where you rest, relax, and play.

Be Known for the Right Stuff.   You have a reputation. You may not have wanted a reputation and you probably didn't expect to have one, but it still exists. You may be known as the office joker, the guy with bad breath, or the office slut—and sadly, it doesn't matter if it's true. It's your reputation. I suggest you try to create a reputation before one is assigned to you. And my suggestion is that you be known as the person who gets things done.

I have a reputation for being an asshole. I can assure you it is a well-earned reputation. I even do what I can to perpetuate it. However, the reputation of being a pain didn't come about because I lie, am dishonest, don't deliver a high-quality product, show up late, am discourteous or lazy. My reputation is because I do what I say I am going to do when I said I would, and I refuse to compromise quality or ethics for any reason. I won't be late and I won't tolerate anyone else being late. I won't lie and I won't tolerate being lied to. I deliver the best possible product I can to the best of my ability every time and I expect the same from those who do business with me. This makes me a total pain to do business with because I have a standard by which I perform and I expect those who do business with me to perform to the same standard. Because of this, I am known as an asshole. Better to get this reputation for the right reasons instead of the wrong reasons.

Get the Hard Stuff Out of the Way First. It's kind of like being a little kid and having to clean your plate. If you are smart, you learn to eat the broccoli first and save the macaroni and cheese for later. The same applies to work. Do the stuff that isn't your favorite when you first get there. Don't put it off. Just get it done, get it out of the way, and move on to the stuff you enjoy.

Stay Focused. Do one job until completion when at all possible. Figure out the most important thing that has to be done today. Then do it. If it really has to be done, you will have accomplished something meaningful regardless of what else doesn't get done. Focus on things of real importance and let the less important things slide. No one ever gets in trouble for doing the things that really matter. The things that really matter produce results that really matter, and we are all measured on the quality of our results, not the quality of our activities.

Don't Be the Cheapest, Be the Best. Don't make it your goal to be the cheapest. Make it your goal to be the best. People who only shop price are not good customers. Companies that sell only on price are rarely good companies to buy from. Anyone can offer you a product or service for a nickel less. And any company can lower their price. But when you give up money, you give up something else: quality, service, or a piece of your integrity. Don't underestimate the customer's willingness to pay more in order to get more. Peace of mind, confidence, buyer satisfaction, and pride in ownership are worth money that many are willing to pay.

Treat People Better Than You Are Willing to Be Treated.
The golden rule is wrong. Don't just treat people the way you want to be treated. Treat them better. Your level of expectation might be pretty low. My expectation when doing business with others is sometimes very low. (I go to restaurants and if the food even shows up, I have a party.) Therefore, you might be willing to accept a lower quality of service than your customer is willing to accept. Don't judge what others want by what you are willing to accept. Err on the side of more. Give more than they expect. Be nicer than they expect. Give better service than they expect. Surprise people by going the extra mile.

Don't Be Afraid to Fire People. People don't do their jobs. You see it every day. I know I do. I go into businesses where I have to beg people to answer a question or pay any attention to me. I have to break up conversations between workers in order to get them to take my order and my money. People take breaks twice as long as they are entitled to. They come in late. They call in sick when they aren't. And they don't get fired. Why? Why do we let people get by with not doing their job? Fear. We are afraid. We spend so much time and money worrying about the rights of the employee that we forget about the rights of the business. If an employee isn't doing his job—isn't earning his money—isn't doing what he is paid to do—he has no rights. Fire him.

Keeping a bad employee destroys your credibility with your other employees. Bad behavior then spreads like a cancer because there are no visible consequences. This is inexcusable because ultimately the person who suffers most is the person who should suffer least: the customer.

"But what if I fire him and he sues me?" You are right about this one. He might sue you. We have become a big sue-happy society. People sue for everything. Get a paper cut? Sue the bastards for unsafe working environment. Someone compliment your outfit? Sue for sexual harassment because obviously, "Nice dress" really meant, "Let's have sex." So yes, you might get sued. Fire him anyway. Remember, it's better to pay a really good attorney than a really bad employee.

Do the Right Thing No Matter What. Ethics is a matter of black and white, not grey. It's either right or wrong, good or bad. How will you know whether something is the right thing to do or the wrong thing to do? If you have to ask, it's the wrong thing. You always know the right thing, you only question when it is the wrong thing. So do the right thing. Even when it is unpopular or might cost you money or be embarrassing. In the long run, consistently doing the right thing will pay off every time.

Positive Attitude at Work. I've already talked about this one many times but it applies to the workplace as well. The Happy Trainers love to tell you the importance of a positive attitude in the workplace. Okay. I guess it's important. But I'll take Mr. Crappy Attitude who gets the work done, and you can have Mr. Positive who believes that there are no problems, only opportunities. I'll go with the guy who knows a problem when he sees it, gets ticked off by it, and solves the problem! I don't want someone around who is so negative that he brings others down, but I'll take some realism over a pair of rose-colored glasses any day.

You Can't Get a Good Deal from a Bad Guy. This is a biggy. I have tried to get a good deal from a bad guy and it just can't be done. Bad people became bad because they do bad things. Don't fall victim to thinking you can be the one person who is going to get a good deal. And if you try but get burned, it's your fault, not theirs. I once tried to sell a guy a house and when we signed the deal, it didn't feel right. He had a smarmy feel about him. But I was desperate to sell. Sure enough, the deal fell apart, I lost money, and it got ugly. I learned a couple of lessons. First, follow your gut. If the deal doesn't feel right, don't do it. Second, a snake will always try to bite you. Don't blame the snake—it is only following its nature. Blame yourself for being willing to get close to it.

Friends and Family Pay Full Retail. When I was in the business of selling telephone systems, a friend of mine asked me to bid on installing a new system in his office. I gave him the price and then, because he was my very good friend, I offered him a discount. He politely turned it down and said he wanted to pay full retail. I asked him why and he told me if he paid full retail, if there were a problem he would have paid for the right to complain. If he got a discount, he forfeited that right. I learned a great lesson that day. By the way, you can use this line when doing business with friends or family. Tell them you want to reserve for them the right to gripe about the service or the product by paying full retail.

Employees Don't Have to Be Happy. I have employees and I don't care whether they are happy or not. I don't pay them to be happy. I pay them to do the job. Know what? They don't care if I am happy, either. They just want me to do my job so they can get paid. It's not about being happy. It's about getting the job done. Besides, I learned a long time ago that I couldn't make another person happy. I can't be happy enough to make them happy. I can't get mad enough or sad enough to make them happy. People are happy *when* they want to be and *if* they want to be. No other person has any impact on it. Besides, it is the job of every employee to make sure the customer is happy whether you are happy or not!

Apathy Is Killing Our Businesses. Employees don't care whether they serve the customer well or even if they serve the customer at all. Managers don't care enough to make sure employees are serving customers or doing their job. And customers don't care enough to complain because they are confident not much will change even when they do. Want things to change? Care. As a customer, care enough to complain. As a manager, care enough to make sure your employees are doing their job. As an employee, care enough to serve the customer well and do your job.

The Number-One, Most Important, Get-This-or-Fail Short Lesson for Both Work and Business. Do what you say you are going to do, when you said you were going to do it, in the way you said you were going to do it. No excuses. No pointing the finger of blame elsewhere. No nothing! Just keep your word. Period. Be the person your co-workers and your customers can put their trust, faith, and confidence in—without exception.

> **Do what you say you are going to do, when you said you were going to do it, in the way you said you were going to do it.**

This is exactly what your customers want from you. This is exactly what you want from your employees and what every employee wants from their employer. This is what your kids want from you and what you want from your kids. It isn't only my number-one rule for work and business but my number-one rule for life itself. This statement sums it all up. It contains all of the rules of customer service, sales, leadership, being a good employer/employee, and even a parent or spouse. If you don't get anything else from this book or any of my books, get this one.

CHAPTER SEVENTEEN

YOU ARE OUT OF TIME

"There is never enough time!"

Well, for once we almost agree on something. It does seem that there is never enough time. And it seems there is less time every day. I am a victim of this one just like you. I need more time. I want more time. There is too much to do and just not enough time to get it all done.

What to do, what to do? I know! Go to a time management seminar. Or buy an organizer and carry it with you all the time so you can plot and plan every moment of every day. Or synch your online calendar with your smartphone! Those things will surely work and you'll have more time. Yeah, right!

TIME MANAGEMENT IS A JOKE

Saying that always upsets my friends who teach time management. It was even called the reason no one should buy this book in one of the reviews of the earlier edition of this book. Good. I'm glad it upsets folks, because I am right and all of them are dead wrong. People are wrong for attempting to teach you how to manage your time. Time cannot be managed. Stop trying. It will only frustrate you. Forget about having the time or not having the time. There is nothing you can do to get more of it anyway, so give it up. Different approach, huh?

Instead of focusing on how much time you have, or don't have, give up focusing on time completely. Instead, begin to focus on priorities instead of time. The problem is never a lack of time; the problem is poorly defined priorities. When you have established the most important thing in the world for you to do, then time will take care of itself.

If I came to your house, opened your garage door, and began to look at your messy garage, like most people you would probably say you have been meaning to clean the place but you have just been too busy. Wrong. You haven't been too busy at all. You didn't clean your garage because it wasn't a priority to you. If it had been a priority you would have found the time to clean it. Our priorities almost always get done because we both find the time and make the time for them. On the other hand, the things that are not all that important to us we let slide.

> **Your time, your energy, and your money always go to what's important to you.**

This idea applies to every area of your life. If I gave you a book that, if you read it and then implemented the principles it talked about, would guarantee you more success, money, and happiness in your life, would you read it? If you are this far in this book, then the answer is obviously yes. But do you actually know why you are reading it? Are you reading this book because there is nothing else you could be doing? No. You are reading it because making your life better is a priority to you. You have made success, happiness, and prosperity priorities and are now doing something to make those things happen. If those things weren't important to you, you would never have cracked the book open.

Even though you are a busy person—and I know you are—you were able to either find the time or make the time to read this book. Other people say they want more success, happiness, and prosperity and they will never find the time to read this book or any other book for that matter. Even though they may have bought the book, they will still not read it. And their excuse will be they have just not had the time to do it. Why? Success, happiness, and prosperity are not priorities to them. Watching television six hours a day or updating their Facebook page—those were their priorities. Plenty of time for those things and absolutely no time to read a book. And they wonder why they aren't doing well? Doing well isn't a priority to them.

Too busy to clean the garage? To play with your kids? To read a book? To call your mom? To go to a movie or to dinner with your spouse? How about if I called and offered you a round of golf at the best course in town for free? Would you be too busy for that? If you were a golfer, you would find the time. You would make the time, because that round of golf would have become a priority to you. If I told you I would give you $5,000 to clean your house completely, play for two hours with your kids, read a book, have dinner with your family, and spend a quality evening with your spouse, along with calling your family to catch up and you only had 24 hours to do it, could you do it? Sure you could! Simply because the $5,000 was important enough to you to make sure you got it all done.

Establish Priorities

Do you have things in your life that need to be done—things that you really want to see accomplished—yet you just haven't been able to find the time to get them done? Right now face the fact those things are never going to get done until they become a priority to you. Figure out what is really important to you. In other words, establish priorities.

Is it your health? If it is, then you will know it's a priority when you do things that make you healthier like eating a proper diet and exercising regularly. Nothing will stand in your way. Not your work, your favorite television show, or any other excuse.

There will be enough time for you to get healthy because you will make enough time to get healthy.

Is your priority to spend more time with your family? If it is, then you will know it's when you start saying no to the things you have been doing and begin to make time for them. Nothing will stand in your way because you have made spending time with your family a priority.

Is having a financially secure future important to you? Check your savings account balance and your investments and your credit card statements and track your spending to find out if that is really true. Chances are that living the "good life" right now is more of a priority than long-term financial security. Fix that now by making your future more of a priority than the present moment.

Reality. In life sometimes the things you don't want to do have to be your priority. Things like picking up the kids, meeting the repairman, and accomplishing your list of honey-do's. I would rather take a beating than meet a repairman. They are never on time and rarely call to advise they will be late; they usually have to come back a second time because they don't have the right things with them to do the job the first time. All of that drives me insane! Yet, life dictates that I sometimes have to do it. Been there? Life is full of have-to's. There is no way around it. I have them. You have them. Things that we are not wild about doing but still have to do. Welcome to life. The key is to figure out how to get them done and still have time to do what you want to do, right?

Just please stop saying there isn't enough time. There is plenty of time to do what is really important to you. Stop being frustrated and get in control. Yes, time is short, and as we age it seems to get shorter. But there will never be enough time to do everything there is to do. However, there is plenty of time to do the things you really want to do. If you want it badly enough you will find the time or make the time.

Don't Watch Your Watch

I love watches. I have several. But I think of them more as jewelry than as timepieces. One reason is that when I hit 50, I could not see the watch face too well so I rarely knew what time it was anyway. And the little date window on the watch face? What a joke! The reason I don't pay that much attention to my watch any longer is something my dad said many times as I was growing up: "We don't wear a watch to know what time it is, we wear a watch to know what time it isn't." He was so right! Do you really ever care what time it is? Now hold on; don't answer too quickly. Don't start yelling, "Well, of course I care what time it is! I have appointments, planes to catch, things to do, people to see." Big deal—we all do. How busy you are doesn't impress me or anyone else. So hang on and let me explain. Do you look at your watch to see if it's time to leave for your appointment or to see if it isn't yet time to leave for your appointment? I bet it's the latter. We don't care what time it *is*, we only care what time it *isn't*. It isn't time to go to lunch. It isn't time to go to the airport. It isn't time for bed. It isn't time to go to work.

And if it isn't time to do those things, there must still be time to do something else. That's what you really want, right? Time to do something else. Time enough to get another cup of coffee. Time enough to relax a little longer. Time to do what you want to do instead of what you have to do.

So what time is it? Time to do the most important thing that needs to be done.

If the most important thing gets done, regardless of what it is, nothing else really matters much.

CHAPTER EIGHTEEN

CHANGE—GET USED TO IT

Change bothers people. In fact, most people hate change. The very idea of changing their routines or habits makes their poor little hearts beat harder. Usually, it's because they are so comfortable in the rut they have dug that even if they are headed down the wrong path, they will stay on it because it doesn't involve any change.

People sit in a room they hate because they don't have the energy or the inclination to change the furniture around or to paint the room. People are afraid to look in the mirror or step on the scale because they know they are overweight, and to change their results they would have to change the way they eat. I know people who are afraid to go to the doctor for fear of finding something wrong, simply because it would change their lifestyle. This list could go on and on. You can think of dozens of ways people you know fear change. You probably even have areas in your life that you are afraid to change.

As for me, I love change. I routinely move my offices every couple of years. I move houses a lot too. I used to buy a new house and move every two years when I could talk my wife into it. I have lived in my current house for eight years, which is nearly an all-time record for me. But I plan on changing that soon.

Change is exciting to me. It gives me a chance to clean up and clean out and to go to work on a new space. It's like starting over physically and psychologically. I make changes in my personal life as well. I like to try new things and go new places and do things I haven't done before.

However, the reality is that most people won't change—even when they know they should. Why? Lots of reasons. Fear is certainly one of them. Years ago I read a great little book called *Feel The Fear . . . And Do It Anyway*, by Susan Jeffers. Read the book when you can, but just internalize the title for right now. You are going to be afraid when facing anything new. No way around it. I am afraid quite a bit of the time. Yep, even me. When I appeared on CNBC's *The Millionaire Inside* as "one of the world's leading money mentors" along with David Bach, Jennifer Openshaw, Keith Ferrazzi, and Robert Kiyosaki, I felt some fear. I am totally confident when I walk on stage to give a speech no matter who the group is or how big the crowd is or what topic I am going to speak about. I never think twice about it. When I was shooting my show, *Big Spender*, I was always confident in what I was going to do and I never broke a sweat over the experience. However, this was different. I was in a foreign environment with renowned experts, and I was going to need to hold my own on the topic of money. My heart was beating a little hard. Despite the internal questions I had about my ability, I walked out on that stage with confidence, grabbed a stool, and did quite well. In fact, looking back at it all, I was pretty amazing. I was scared but I blew through the fear and conquered the situation. I felt the fear, but I did it anyway.

While I am often afraid of what I have to do, I am even more afraid of not doing it. In my *New York Times* bestseller, *People Are Idiots and I Can Prove It*, I wrote about the 10 ways people sabotage their lives, with one of those being "Not Recognizing Consequences." Every action has a consequence. Some have positive consequences and some have negative consequences. Some consequences are slow to feel and some are immediate. But just as every action has a consequence, every non-action also has a consequence.

If there are no immediate external consequences for non-performance, I create my own. No, I don't punish myself or ground myself for not doing something. I just create the consequence of disappointment. I am disappointed when I don't achieve what I set out to achieve. However, not when I've done my best. I never beat myself up for doing my best. I am only disappointed in myself when I have done less than my best. And not doing my best is usually the reason I didn't accomplish what I set out to do.

However, the real disappointment for me is when I don't achieve something simply because I have been too afraid to even give it a shot.

> **To begin a journey and not make it is forgivable.**
> **Not to begin the journey at all is unforgivable.**
> **What is the worst that could happen?**

This is the question I always ask myself when I am afraid to do something. If the worst that can happen is, "I'm going to die," then I don't do it. But that is rarely the answer to anything I am going to attempt. Usually the worst that can happen is that I won't do as well as I had hoped for. Or I might embarrass myself. Is that really so bad? Even if I do it and do it badly, it's better than if I had never attempted it. So I go for it.

You aren't going to die from going after more success, happiness, and prosperity either. Ask yourself, "What's the worst that could happen?" Then go for it. Besides, the worst thing that could happen rarely happens anyway.

Dara Torres, the swimmer, won a Silver Medal during the 2008 Olympics at the age of 41. I watched her in an interview with Matt Lauer where the topic was her age in comparison to other Olympic contenders. She said, "The water doesn't know what age you are so just jump in and go for it." The same applies to you as well. Life doesn't know, or care, how old you are or what other excuse you are clinging to, so just jump in and go for it.

Don't worry that you don't know everything. Don't get caught up in what might happen or might not happen. Don't be paralyzed by fear. Don't concern yourself with what others think. In fact, don't over-think the decision at all. When an antelope hears a lion roar, he doesn't continue to graze and think about whether he should run or not. He runs like hell because his very life depends on it. No thought is involved. He instinctually moves. Become like the antelope, because the lion is roaring and your very life depends on it. Move.

Do you know of changes you need to make in your life? Chances are you do. Then follow these simple ideas and get started. Face your fear and do it anyway.

CHAPTER NINETEEN

HOT TOPICS

CHILL

You know, relax. I'm not very good at relaxing. I'm certainly better at it than I used to be, but still not as good at it as I should be. I don't have much time at home and it's hard for me to gear down after several days on the road. I get a little frustrated knowing I have to squeeze all of the things I want to do at home into the few days I have. I always feel rushed, and rushed isn't relaxed. Plus, my brain is always busy. I don't know how people can just go blank and not think about stuff but it's hard for me. I am always thinking about the book I am writing or the next television appearance or blog I'm about to write or . . . the list goes on and on.

For me and many others, the ability to relax has to be learned. That's not a problem for everyone for sure, since there are millions who have no problem sitting on their butt not doing a damn thing. I don't know how they do it. I'm just not comfortable when I'm doing nothing.

I've learned one of the key ingredients for being able to relax is to really enjoy where you live—both the city and the house. I live in Paradise Valley, Arizona. I love Arizona. I find the desert peaceful and relaxing and I enjoy the heat. I also love my house. I like it so much I get jealous of my wife who gets to enjoy it all by herself with just my dogs when I am gone.

Create an environment you can enjoy and relax in, even if it's just one room. My office is that way. I am surrounded by things I enjoy: lots of books, cigar store Indians, Elvis decanters, movie posters, and pictures of people I love. I am completely comfortable and creative there. When I'm home I spend a lot of time there. Do your best to make a personal space you can love. Just one room, or even just a corner in the room, or a chair—a place where you can let the world go away.

Another way to relax is to find something you enjoy as an outlet. For some it's golf or fishing—some sort of physical exercise. For others it's reading or sewing. For some, great music or movies. I'm lucky that I like to do a lot of things. I can throw paint on a canvas and my mind just goes to another place. I like to play golf and I absolutely love going out into the desert or the woods and riding my ATV. I find when I do these things that my face automatically ends up in a smile, the crinkles in my forehead go away, and my mind is totally in the moment with little thought of what else is going on in my world. Find something that makes you feel that way—an activity that relaxes your mind.

Another thing you can do to relax is to schedule days (at least one day) when you have nothing going on. I mean nothing. No repair guys to interrupt your day, to show up late, and to end up breaking more than they fix. No lunches with friends. No honey-do's. Nothing. And that kind of day must be scheduled. Then you must be firm about keeping to the schedule of nothingness. Can't do a day? Set aside an hour. An hour to sit with no interruptions.

The other thing you have to learn to do in order to relax is . . . Sorry, I don't know what the other thing is. See, I told you I was not very good at this.

STRESS: WHO NEEDS IT?

Ooooooh, this is a biggy. People love to talk about how stressed out they are.

"Life is just so stressful."

"My kids are stressing me out."

"The holidays are such a stressful time."

"I just can't—I'm so stressed."

"My boss causes me so much stress!"

Heard that stuff? Said that stuff? I am sick of it!

I have colleagues who make their living doing stress management seminars. Ever been to one? What a waste. Why would you want to learn how to manage something you don't need at all?

I'll tell you what I have learned about stress. It has been one of my major life lessons: Stress comes from knowing what is right and doing what is wrong.

Stress comes from knowing what is right and doing what is wrong.

Got that highlighter handy? Mark that line right now because you need to remember it.

Take a sheet of paper and write down some of the things you believe to be causing you stress. Go ahead, stop right now; get a pen and paper and do it.

Now look at your list. You know exactly the right thing to do about each of the things on your list. Yes, you do. Don't argue with me. Regardless of what you wrote down, you know. In fact, you have probably known for a good long while what you should do, but you simply haven't done it.

The problem is that you are either doing nothing or you are doing the wrong thing. That's what is causing the stress. It isn't the things you wrote down that are causing the stress at all. It's that you know the right thing to do about them and you just aren't doing it.

For instance, if you're like most of the people who have done this exercise with me in my seminars, you probably wrote down a person's name at the top of your stress list. Maybe it was your spouse, or one of your kids who is driving you crazy. It might even be an employee or co-worker who is causing you stress.

You know what you ought to do about that person. You ought to dump them. Or you might need to apologize to them. Or you ought to tell them you love them. Or you need to fire them. Regardless of the action you need to take, know that the person isn't the cause of the stress. The stress you are feeling is caused by you not doing what you know is the right thing to do.

Maybe you wrote down the thing I find to be one of the most popular causes of stress: your weight. Again, you know exactly the right thing to do about your weight. Stop eating like a pig. Start exercising. Very simple. Your weight isn't causing you any stress at all. The stress you feel is caused by the fact you know you need to stop eating like a pig and you should get off your butt and exercise, and you are not doing it!

See how it works? Go through this process with each of the things on your list. Then deal with what you know is the right thing to do. Take the action you know in your gut you need to take. It may be painful, expensive, or even embarrassing. It probably won't be easy and will make you uncomfortable. However, as hard as it may be to deal with, it will still be much easier than living with the stress.

Guilt Serves No Purpose

"But what am I supposed to feel when I do something I am sorry for?"

Good question. Easy answer: regret.

It's natural to have some regret when you've made a mistake. That isn't guilt. We all make mistakes and feel bad about it. That is regret. Regret means you're sorry and you don't intend to repeat the same action again. That's a good emotion as it motivates you to better behavior. Guilt, however, is an emotion that can easily immobilize you. That's why guilt serves no purpose. It won't help you in any way. It's a waste of time. You can't change what has been done by feeling guilty about it.

The past is just that: passed. Gone. Slipped away. Not to be repeated again. If you need to make restitution, do it. If you messed up, apologize. If you are forgiven for your mistake, give thanks and move on. If you are not forgiven for the mistake you made, then move on anyway. Forgive yourself, learn from the experience, and act differently next time. At that point, it's over.

Worry Is a Waste of Time

There are only two areas of life: the things you can control and the things you can't control. Why worry about what you can't control? How stupid is that? If you can control it, then why worry about it? After all, it's in your control, thus making worry a total waste of energy.

The past is something you cannot control. It's over. Don't worry about it. The future is something you can control. But there is no need to worry about the future either. The present should be your only concern as it's the only thing under your control. Live the present the way you know you should live it, doing the right thing in each situation, and the future will take care of itself.

This is a hard thing to do, I know. My son was in Baghdad during Operation Iraqi Freedom. I hated it. Like all of the families of our men and women in the service, I was scared to death for him. But there wasn't one thing I could do about it. It was his job. A job he enjoyed and had volunteered to do, so it was beyond my control. My worry about him did him no good and it was wrecking my sanity. So I reminded myself of my own credo to forget worry. Worry is a misuse of your imagination. Worry attracts to you exactly what you don't want to happen. Because I know this to be true about worry, I gave it up. Instead I turned my energy toward him coming home safely. I put my energy into the outcome I wanted, instead of the outcome I did not want. My son is back home now and is a cop. He still faces dangerous situations every day. People often ask me, "Aren't you scared to death for him?" My answer is, "What good would that do? Would my being afraid for him make him safer?"

Stop focusing on what you don't want to happen. In other words, stop worrying. Instead, stay focused on what you want to happen. Focus your energy and your efforts on the kind of life you want, the relationships you want and the stuff you want.

Selfishness Is a Good Thing

You have been told your whole life not to be selfish, but the people who told you that were dead wrong. You should share your money and your stuff and your talents—I have already addressed that. However, you have to learn to be selfish with yourself. Your first obligation is to yourself. You can't be any good for someone else unless you are first good to yourself.

Be selfish with your time. Learn to say no to things you don't want to do and have no interest in out of some insincere sense of obligation. You aren't serving anyone when you spread yourself too thin. Say no to the things that keep you from saying yes to what you really want to do and should be doing. Say no to going to some stupid get-together you don't want to go to and will be full of people you care nothing about so you can say yes to spending some quality time with your family. That form of selfishness is the best kind. The selfishness to put your real priorities ahead of someone else's priorities for you.

Be selfish with your helpfulness. Am I saying to stop being helpful? Absolutely not. I'm just saying to give your help whole-heartedly to those who *want* it, but selfishly to those who *need* it. Many people need help—we all recognize that. But many of those who need help really don't want it. So do both of you a favor and don't help them. People who need help rarely appreciate it when it's given, and rarely do anything with the help that's given anyway. Don't waste your time. Instead, help people who sincerely want to be helped. They will appreciate it and actually use the help given them. Remember, people change when they want to, not when you want them to. And people turn around when they want to, not when they need to.

A Deal Is a Deal

This is an old saying I know you have heard many times, so whatever happened to living up to it?

Remember the movie *Indecent Proposal* with Robert Redford, Demi Moore, and Woody Harrelson? Redford offers a million bucks to spend one night with Demi (not a bad investment if you ask me). Demi and Woody are newlyweds with money problems and agree to take the million, and off she trots to spend the night with Redford (not a bad deal for Demi, if you ask my wife). Then poor old Woody goes ape! Hey Woody, a deal is a deal. Grow up.

We've all made mistakes of overpromising—your mouth often overloads your ass, as the saying goes. So? What difference should that make? What does any of it have to do with the fact that you made a commitment and now are expected to live up to it? So you overpromised and now are not happy about it. A deal is a deal. Suck it up and keep your word.

Yes, it might cost you some money to live up to your word. Yes, it might be painful to deliver on your promise. Yes, it might be embarrassing to you or humiliate you. It might be expensive or inconvenient. Tough! A deal is a deal. Make a better deal next time—be smarter next time—but this time live up to your commitment.

If you make a promise, keep it. If you give your word, don't go back on it. If you say you are going to be there at a certain time, be there. If you mess up, admit it and accept the consequences. If you are paid for a service, provide that service when you said you would and exactly as you said you would. Any less than this makes you a liar. Harsh? Too bad. I warned you I was going to be harsh, and after all: A deal is a deal.

Less Gray, More Black and White

Some folks have some issues with my black and white approach to self-improvement, finances, parenting, business, and life in general. They love to point out that there are several areas that really are gray when it comes to life. No kidding? Thanks for pointing that out to me. I had no idea that was the case. How could I know that? I have never had a problem or faced a challenge. I have never raised teenagers, had money issues, been married or divorced, held a job, managed people, driven down the street, eaten out, bought anything, had a bill, or had to make a tough decision. Never. None of those things. I have lived a completely sheltered life in a cave blessed with only positive thoughts and outcomes. I have attracted all of my success through *The Secret* and *The Law of Attraction*. I have never had a real life facing all of the things real people face, and I honestly had no idea that life had any gray areas.

Come on folks, I know life is full of gray areas. It's just that I think we have all become way too comfortable living in those gray areas. Gray areas used to be little tiny corners we could escape to in order to justify our stupid actions and results. Now the gray areas are everywhere! Our homes, our businesses, our government, our society, our grocery stores, in our books, and all over our televisions. Our leaders spew gray and drape it in red, white, and blue. Things are so gray that when someone actually draws a line and paints one side black and the other side white, it bothers the hell out of people! We have become comfortable and embraced the gray areas way too much and shied away from the uncomfortable realities of black and white. I want people to begin to think more in terms of black and white. Right or wrong. People need to understand they are either doing enough or they aren't doing enough. We need to recognize we are either giving our best or we aren't. You are either on the way, or you are in the way. You are either living within your means or you aren't. It's either the truth or it's a lie.

It's easier to live in the black and white world. That's why I am so confused by those who love the gray area so much. When faced with a decision, you just make it quickly based on whether it's the right thing to do or the wrong thing to do. You don't have to wallow in it, meditate on it, study it, consider it, hold a focus group, or take a vote. You simply do the right thing.

Why? Because you can. All it takes is some guts. A backbone. A pair.

You will be criticized for it. Trust me, I know. Who cares? You will be given grief at work for kissing up by doing your job when others are slacking. Tell them to kiss off. Your friends will give you crap about being too tough on your kids. They will laugh at you for saying no to spending money when you know you can't afford it. They will ridicule you for not taking the easy road when you know you should take the right road. Those people are not your friends—dump them. Now. And never look back.

Do the right thing in your life every time to the best of your ability. You won't be perfect at it. I'm certainly not. I mess up every day and slip and slide around in the gray area, just like everyone else. But every day, I remind myself I can do a little better; take more of a stand for what I know is right, and take action on it. That's all it takes: a decision to do it, a willingness to take action, the humility to admit you aren't doing your best, the honestly to confront yourself for it, and the willingness to keep on doing what you know is right regardless of the consequences. Yep, that's it: It's black or white.

Forget Passion

When I appeared on CNBC's "The Big Idea with Donny Deutsch," I made the statement, "Passion is a load of crap." Poor Donny grew pale under his stage make-up and his heart pounded hard while he gasped for air. To say the least, he disagreed. My point to him was that passion is little more than a starting place, but true long-term success is based on excellence and hard work. Again, he disagreed. That's fine. He has the right to be wrong. And he clearly is.

I know many passionate people. They are passionately stupid, passionately wrong, and passionately incompetent. Passion and success have about as much to do with each other as gravy and Raisin Bran. But this is the trash being dumped on us by the ill-informed motivational idiots who know little about true success but are quick to tell you how to achieve it. No business ever makes it based on passion. No successful businessperson ever made it to the top based on passion.

Success isn't about passion. Success is about the combination of hard work and excellence. Yes, the combination of the two. Excellence isn't enough. I see people who are excellent at what they do but don't work hard enough to ever become successful. Hard work isn't enough either. There are people who work very hard but simply aren't any good at what they do.

Telling people that passion is the key to success does folks a great disservice. Because somewhere down the road, they will discover that no one cares about or shares their passion. They will find out that while they are passionate, they haven't put in the time or effort in order to be really good at what they do. They know nothing about selling or marketing, leadership, man-agement, finance, their competition, serving customers, or all the other facets of a successful life or business. All they have is their passion. Try cashing that at the bank.

Standing on a stage thousands of miles away from home and going back to a crappy hotel room only to eat one more room service Cobb salad is nothing that creates any passion in me. It's my job. I'm good at it and I like it. Plus, it pays well. My being good at it is why people hire me. If I was only passionate and not amazing at it, no one would ever hire me. And if I didn't work hard at making sure I got booked to do the speeches, my business would go broke. Same with the books—it's a combination of hard work and excellence—not passion—that makes them good and helps them sell.

Passion might qualify me to stand on the street corner and preach my message, but it wouldn't allow me to make a living. Excellence gets me paid. And years of hard work, study, and practice made me excellent. The same applies to you. Set your passion aside and get really good at what you do. Got it? Forget what you are hearing about passion and just go to work.

Don't Take the Easy Way

It's easier to be stupid than it is be smart. That's because being smart takes a little effort. It's work to find the truth out about any issue, so it's easier to just accept what you hear as fact.

It's easier to listen to the political pundits and television news anchors and trust their words completely than it is to study, read, and search to discover the truth about a political issue or to actually read one of the bills or proposals you are so vehemently for or against. It's easier to listen to the preachers and believe every word they say from their pulpit than it is to read the book yourself, or maybe lots of books and search for your own insight and develop your beliefs based on your own experiences. It's easier to just toe the party line because you are registered Democrat or Republican or Green Party or Tea Party or Whatever Party than it is to ask whether the party line even makes any sense or not.

It's easier to believe your doctor when he tells you that you should take a pill rather than to do some research or get a second opinion to find out if he knows what he is talking about or whether he is padding his pocket and those of the pharmaceutical companies. It's easier to buy a pill or have surgery to lose the pounds than it is to start eating right and doing some exercise.

It's easier to steal a car than it is to get a job, earn money, build credit, and buy a car.

It's easier to charge something than it is to pay cash.

It's easier to blame than to take responsibility.

Bottom line: It's just easier to be stupid and do stupid things.

Smart people take responsibility for their lives. They require a lot from themselves and from others. Smart people work hard and pay their bills. Smart people are good parents. Smart people are concerned about their health and the health of their family.

The argument from many is going to be that there are many smart people who aren't good parents. Or that there are smart people who don't work hard or pay their bills. Or that there are plenty of smart people who are obese. You can't sell me on that argument. These people might be considered intelligent, but they aren't smart, they are stupid. Being smart requires that you do the right thing or at least work at trying to do the right thing.

We are a society which loves to brag about how smart we are. But are we? It doesn't appear so on many fronts. Being smart requires that we be responsible, and that simply isn't the case for most people. We require almost nothing of ourselves that involves any real work, effort, or sacrifice.

The Bible says "to whom much is given, much is required." And each of us has been given a lot.

We have been given a great planet to live on, yet we stupidly spend most of our day destroying it. After all, it's work to conserve. It requires sacrifice. Not big sacrifices for sure, but even a small sacrifice requires more of us than no sacrifice. "Give up my gas guzzler? No way!" "Put in energy conserving light bulbs? They cost a dollar more!" "Turn up my thermostat two degrees? What? I've earned the right to be as cool as I want to be!"

We have been given a job, yet few people do more than what is minimally required of them in order to keep their job and draw their check. After all, giving your best requires integrity, and it's easier to live without integrity than with it.

We have been given great kids, yet we don't communicate with them, spend much time with them, or set good examples for them.

We are given great civil liberties, yet few people vote or become involved.

Most of us were given health, yet we ate our way, smoked our way, and lazied our way out of that great gift.

We have been given the opportunity to accomplish great things, yet we squander that opportunity by sitting on our ass and watching mindless drivel on the television.

We have been given all the keys to success, happiness, and prosperity but only a few will ever bother to read the books that hold those keys.

Instead, we take the easy way out. The stupid way out. Because anything else would require effort and few are willing to put in the effort to change their lives or their circumstances. Instead, they would rather just complain about the hand they have been dealt and their lot in life. They would rather bitch about the government or gripe about the stupidity of others rather than own up to their own laziness and inaction. They would rather blame the economy or Wall Street rather than own up to the fact that they overspent and never saved. They would rather blame their boss than own up to the fact that they called in sick when they weren't and took longer breaks than allowed and gave 75 percent effort instead of 100 percent. They would rather blame the school system than realize that they never spent any time with their kids making sure they could add or read or spell. They would rather blame the government for squandering their tax dollars than admit that they cheated on their own income taxes.

Being given much really does mean that much is required of you. It means that if you have money, you are required to do the right thing with your money, including saving, investing, spending, and being charitable. It means that if you have kids you are required to talk to them, spend time with them, teach them, and set a good example for them. It means that if you have a job you are required to give it your best for no other reason than that you were hired to do so. It also means that if you are smart, you are required to use your smarts in ways that serve yourself, your family, and others in responsible ways. And that requires work.

That's why it's easier to be stupid—it doesn't really require any work.

I will readily admit that I often do take the easy way out myself. I find it easier to *not* do something than it is to do something. I try not to get caught in that trap often, and I try not to let it spread like a cancer into all areas of my life. I try to recognize it quickly, correct it even quicker, and get back on track immediately. But it still happens and I still offer myself excuses for it. Bottom line: There is no excuse. Doing the easy thing is rarely about doing the right thing. If the wind is at your back, you are going in the wrong direction.

Success Is a Balancing Act

Years ago I came up with my personal definition of success:

> **Success is being all you can be in each area of your life without sacrificing your ability to be all you can be in each and every other area of your life.**

This definition is based in balance. It makes no sense to be the world's greatest salesperson and have bad health. It's nothing but sad to have made a lot of money but sacrificed your family along the way. Never sacrifice one area over another. I believe, as Tom Hopkins once said, "To be rich and sick is stupid."

While I am a firm believer in balance, I am also very realistic regarding balance and the achievement of success in the various areas of life. In order to achieve balance, you must first become unbalanced. In other words, if you are broke and need money, then you're going to have to become unbalanced in order to make that happen. You aren't going to have the time to relax, or play with the family quite as much, or go to the gym as much. You have to work. I understand that. I even condone that. For a while. Not for long, though. At some point you still have to go back to paying attention to all the other areas of life. That is the challenge. It seems when we focus on our work, we lose perspective and let the other areas of life suffer. Then we become accustomed to not seeing our kids or playing with them, and we get used to not taking care of ourselves physically. And before you know it, you have no relationship with your family and you are sick and tired and lonely and old. Yeah, you are rich and you have a big office, but that is about it. Be careful. Work hard but not so hard that you lose your life.

It works the other way around, too. Play hard. But don't play so hard that you sacrifice your livelihood either. Balance is the key. Think of your life in terms of a wheel with spokes. Each spoke represents the various areas of your life: physical, intellectual, spiritual, social, financial, career, family, fun and play, alone time, friends, and civic responsibility. With each of these areas as the spoke of a wheel, considering your own life, how smooth is the ride? Do all of the spokes hit the ground on a regular basis? Or do you have some flat spots?

Growth in one area of your life means you will let another area slide slightly. But slightly is the operative word. Don't completely abandon any one area in pursuit of another. People who do that, and I am sure you can name a few, are one-dimensional, boring, and end up leading sad, unfulfilled lives. They have cheated themselves, those around them, and the rest of the world by not living life to its fullest in all areas.

CHAPTER TWENTY

WHAT'S REALLY IMPORTANT?

Seems like such an easy question to answer. The average, normal person would quickly say "my kids," or "my family," or "being healthy" and so on. I bet those answers are about what you came up with when you first read the question too.

It's just that I'm not buying those answers. I'm not calling anyone a liar who recites those quick and easy answers; it's just that I don't buy that's what is really important to most people. Why would I say that? Because there isn't too much proof to suggest those answers are the truth.

One of my basic philosophies is that your time, your energy, and your money go to what is important to you. So if kids and family and being healthy were as important as most people say, it would follow that is where people would focus their time, energy, and money. Follow? Well, it isn't happening. Look around and you'll see that people are clearly not putting their actions into the important things in life. People are putting their time, energy, and money into lots of things, but more often than not it's the temporary, the mundane, and the instantly gratifying. The ridiculous occupies people's time, saps their energy, and seduces the money from their fingers. And the media help with that fascination. But I don't blame the media because they only give us what we beg to see. It's not their fault they are capitalizing on our preoccupation with the stupid; it's our own. Watching stupid stuff on television is voluntary participation. No one forces you to sit there and see who the newest stupid celebrity is and what he/she is doing.

You choose to do that. People choose to participate in things of no importance and neglect what is really important. I dealt in great detail about this problem in my book, *The Idiot Factor: The Ten Ways We Sabotage Our Life, Money and Business* (formerly titled *People Are Idiots and I Can Prove It*).

Are there exceptions? Of course there are, so don't get all fired up and write me a bunch of comments about how wrong I am and how my premise doesn't apply to you. Fine. You may be the exception. Read this and be satisfied with how none of this applies to you and find some satisfaction in pointing the finger of blame at everyone else.

"I get it, Larry. So what is important?"

Your obligations are important. What does that entail? Your relationships, your family, your bills and other financial commitments, your employment, and your health. Don't just say "of course" to this statement. Look closely at each of these obligations and consider that the word really means that you are obligated to take care of these things to the very best of your ability. And I don't mean with your words, but with your actions!

You are obligated to do the job you were hired to do. It's not important that you be happy or enjoy it; it's important that you do it. That was the agreement you made when you took the job, so do your job and be thankful you have one because millions of people don't.

You are obligated to be as healthy as you can so you can live as long as you can and not be sick and become a drain on your family physically, mentally, or financially. You owe good health to your family and to yourself.

You are obligated to pay your bills—on time and as agreed to. That is money you gave your word you would pay when the goods or service were extended to you, so pony up and do what's right, even though we are in a recession. Even though money may be tight. Pay your obligations before you do anything else. Don't go to the movies, out to eat, or buy anything other than what it takes to survive; instead, pay your obligations no matter what it takes. That's the important thing to do.

Here is the most important thing and your biggest obligation: your kids. We are a world in crisis. I know it and you know it too. There is no other decent way to describe it: We are in a mess! How did we get in this mess? The mess happened because we either didn't care enough to keep it from happening or we weren't involved enough to know it was happening. Either way, we allowed it to happen. We are to blame. And we have to take responsibility and fix it.

The best, long-term solution to turning our world around is to create a society that knows how to be honest and do the right thing in every situation. No more situational ethics but real ethics based on honesty and integrity. We have to create a society that knows how to earn money, save money, be charitable, invest, and enjoy their money as well. We have to raise kids that grow into adults who know how to give their word, mean it, and keep it. Who do their job for no other reason than because they said they would. Who know how to treat people fairly and be healthy and take care of the environment. Who become involved in their communities and in their world to fix the problems we face. Who know how to take action and work to create change instead of sitting on their butts and griping about the way things are. Raising kids to be and do their best is our obligation as a society. But it's also every parent's obligation. To fail at raising your kids and teaching them how to succeed is the ultimate failure as a person. Good parenting is the most important thing any person can ever do. Nothing will make a bigger difference in our world than people raising kids who will become responsible, productive adults.

This message has become my primary focus and my purpose. It's impossible to fix the problems surrounding business and money without addressing the primary cause. I can't help businesses do better in the future until we create a society that believes in honesty, service, and takes its job seriously. It does little good to talk about money and credit obligations until parents teach their kids about how to earn, save, spend, and honor their commitments. That's the problem right now with people and their money—they weren't taught the things that really matter. That has to change. My work can have no lasting impact on society without going to the source of our problem: bad parenting. It means everything to all of us that we turn our world around, and that is clearly not going to happen with the adults we have in charge of our businesses, our schools, and our governments right now or in the foreseeable future. Which means, it changes with our kids. It changes with your kids.

I ask that you stop and take your obligations seriously. How will you know if you are doing that? Measure the amount of time, energy, and money you put into an activity and that will tell you whether you consider it to be important or not. Pay attention to that especially when it comes to your kids.

CHAPTER TWENTY-ONE

HARD LESSONS TO LEARN

These are the short lessons that are sometimes hard to learn and sometimes even harder to accept. These lessons don't need a chapter to explain them. They don't even need a paragraph. Some lessons are so powerful and so short, you just say them.

- When people tell you how rich they are, chances are they are not.
- When people tell you how intelligent they are, they actually are proving how little they know, not how much they know.
- When people tell you how successful they are, chances are they are not.
- When people tell you what a devout Christian they are, especially more than once, they are usually anything but.
- When people tell you how honest they are, keep your hand on your wallet.
- When people say, "Let me be frank with you," it means in the past they haven't been.
- When people say, "And that's the truth," be skeptical.
- When people say, "Let me tell you this for your own good," it's for their own good, not yours.
- When people say, "I only have one thing to say about that," be prepared for a lot more than one thing to follow.
- When people say, "I'll try," don't count on it.

Source: Larry Winget, "Shut Up, Stop Whining, and Get a Life," SmarterComics.

- Never say anything stupid like, "It just can't get any worse than this!" That is a challenge you don't want to issue to the universe. If there is one thing I have learned in life, it's that it can always get worse.
- There is an old saying that goes, "Kids should be seen and not heard." Actually I think the truer statement would be, "Neighbors should be seen and not heard."
- Rich makes up for a whole lot of ugly.
- The less people have to say, the more they feel compelled to say it, and they probably will use bad grammar and won't be able to spell it.
- Common sense is no longer common. Neither is common knowledge or common courtesy.
- When someone says, "If I had a nickel for every time..." the truth is they would have about 35 cents.

- Keep it simple. When it starts feeling complicated, stop, evaluate, simplify, and begin again.
- Don't worry too much about people liking you. It's better if they respect you.
- Focus on accomplishment, not activity.
- People will almost always lie to protect themselves.
- Never tolerate disrespect from anyone.

CHAPTER TWENTY-TWO

THE TEST FOR SUCCESS

At this point you probably want to know, "If I do all of this stuff, will I be successful?"

Yes, I believe if you do all of this stuff you will be successful. You may not achieve all your wildest dreams, live in Aruba, drive a Rolls, and drink Pina Coladas all day long, never having to lift a finger again, but you will be more successful than you are right now. Remember, success is a sliding scale. You look at where you are, then decide where you want to be. Then you move between where you are to where you want to be. But trust me when I say, once you get there, you are going to want to go further. That's why you never really reach the pinnacle of success; the mountain just keeps growing. But there is still a way to know if you are moving in the right direction. I've put together a little test for you to help you make sure you are headed in the right direction.

Am I happy?
Am I healthy?
Am I serving?
Am I loving?
Am I learning?
Am I having fun?
Am I doing something I enjoy?
Am I prosperous?

Clearly, you can answer yes to one question and no to another. That's to be expected. You can be healthy and broke. But if the answer is yes to even one of these questions, you are successful in that area, so celebrate that level of success. If the answer to any of these questions is no, then stop and do whatever it takes to turn that no into a yes.

GET READY FOR THE ROLLER COASTER RIDE!

Source: Larry Winget, "Shut Up, Stop Whining, and Get a Life," SmarterComics.

Success doesn't mean that you won't have problems or bumps in the road on your journey. If you believe that's the way it works, then you are truly naïve and need to wake up to the reality of life. Life just isn't like that, and actually I don't believe you would really want it to be. Life is more like a roller coaster ride. My grandfather was a carney. I grew up going to the carnival and riding the rides. I always liked the roller coaster. It has its uphill climb that chug-chug-chugs along and fills you with anticipation. It has its downhill runs at breakneck speeds that will terrify you. It has dark, scary tunnels where you scream and become so afraid. There is something not quite completely safe about roller coasters. They feel dangerous. Sometimes you even throw up! But for the most part they leave you laughing hysterically and grabbing the person next to you out of joy and fear and a rush of many emotions.

A roller coaster is never dull because there is something different about to happen all the time. When you get off, you can't wait to get back on and do it again. So you either pay the price of admission and go along for the ride, or you spend your life as an observer, watching the others have all the fun. Or you spend your time waiting in line, and then when it's finally your turn, you step back to let someone else go on ahead of you because you aren't sure you can handle it. Some folks even choose to just skip the roller coaster altogether and instead get on the merry-go-round, where the sweet music plays and you go around in circles. The merry-go-round is nice and sweet and safe, the music is happy, and it's a pleasant experience all around. You're never afraid and you never cry and you never throw up. But you never scream with laughter and you never cry out in terror and you never grab the person next to you out of joy or for comfort.

I have done the merry-go-round and I have ridden the roller coaster. I have made my choice. I choose the roller coaster. There is more risk when you choose the roller coaster, but at least you will know you have lived.

Which one have you been riding?

CHAPTER TWENTY-THREE

A FINAL THOUGHT

You're finished. You've read the book. Good for you.
You are now further along than most people will ever be simply because you finished one book. But does that mean you are finished? Hardly. Reading a book isn't really that impressive and won't do one thing to make your life better, so don't take too much credit too quickly. It takes much more than reading a book for your life to change. So you aren't finished by a long shot. In fact, you're just getting started. Now is when the hard stuff happens for you, because now you have to take some action. Oh yeah, in case you aren't clear on what that means, it means you have to go to work. There's that ugly word again: work!

I hope you will decide to go to work. I hope you will choose to live life differently than you have for one simple reason: You can. Yeah, that is what it comes down to: You change because you can. That should be enough for you right there.

Let me close with an exchange I recently had with a magazine reporter.

He asked me, "Larry, at the end of the day, what really matters?" My answer was, "Not much. Really, not much matters. At the end of the day if you smiled more than you frowned, laughed more than you cried, told your family and friends you loved them, and had a pretty good time doing what you do for a living, then it was a good day. Go to bed and say thanks."

If you don't do the stuff I have suggested in this book, it's fine with me. I don't know you and will never have a clue whether you did any of this stuff or not. So it doesn't matter to me if you change or not. It will matter to your family and to your bank account and when you look in the mirror. What I really want for you is to be able to end every day with the answer I gave that reporter. Because in the end that is what really matters. If you can do those things, you are okay in my books.

"Those are my principles, and if you don't like them, I have more."

—Groucho Marx
